Just Keep Moving

Just Keep Moving

Breaking the Silence while Changing Directions from Despair to Happiness

Sandra Beltran

PYP
Academy
Press

For permission requests, write to the below address:

PYP Academy Press
141 Weston Street, #155
Hartford, CT 06141

The opinions expressed by the Author are not necessarily those held by PYP Academy Press.

Ordering Information: Quantity sales and special discounts are available on quantity purchases by corporations, associations, and others. For details, contact the author at sandra@sandrabeltran.com.

Edited by: Gina Sartirana, Chloë Siennah & Malka Wickramatilake
Cover design by: Nelly Murariu
Typeset by: Medlar Publishing Solutions Pvt Ltd., India

Printed in the United States of America.

ISBN: 979-8-88797-004-2 (hardcover)
ISBN: 979-8-88797-003-5 (paperback)
ISBN: 979-8-88797-005-9 (ebook)

Library of Congress Control Number: 2022917121

First edition, October 2022.

Publish Your Purpose is a hybrid publisher of non-fiction books. Our authors are thought leaders, experts in their fields, and visionaries paving the way to social change—from food security to anti-racism. We give underrepresented voices power and a stage to share their stories, speak their truth, and impact their communities. Do you have a book idea you would like us to consider publishing? Please visit PublishYourPurpose.com for more information.

Dedication

*I dedicate this book to Sophia Ward, my oldest daughter.
From the day she came into my life, she showed me the true
meaning of unconditional love. She has grown to be a fantastically
intuitive, passionate lover of life who exudes compassion.
Thank you for pushing me to be true to myself.*

Table of Contents

Acknowledgments

This book would not be possible if it weren't for the support and encouragement I received from my friend, Pam Jackson, a writer and author of many books. As I began writing this book, I shared a couple of chapters with her, looking for validation. She did more than validate me. She urged me to move forward and tell my story, giving me the initial push I needed.

To Mindy Raymond Benson, my friend who listened to me go on and on about my book. She put me in touch with the folks at Publish Your Purpose, who have been the perfect fit for me.

To my brother, Oscar, who not only was my childhood companion but taught me that humor could help heal. He allowed me to ask questions about our past, opening old wounds and talking through the sequence of events.

To my little sister, Roxanne, who is always there for me, giving me unconditional love and inspiring me to move forward.

To my mother, Rosa; when I told her I was writing a book about our past, she looked at me as if to say, "Oh no, I can only imagine all the bad things you wrote about me," but never said, "Don't do it." Instead, without saying a word, she looked at me with pride and encouragement. Thank you for giving me the strength and resilience to survive this life.

To my friend, Kerry, who reminds me every time I see her how great I am and that I am a gift. True or not, thank you for your belief in me.

Then there is my daughter, Sophia, who would read the pages of this book over my shoulder and be so intrigued by the story, giving me the inspiration I needed to keep going. Thank you for always speaking out about your feelings and letting me know when I'm wrong, even if I don't like it.

To my son, Colin, who challenges me every day to be a good person and keep me true to my word.

And finally, to all my nieces and nephews that have taken the best parts of us and are making a better life for themselves, breaking cycles, and creating healthier life choices for future generations.

Literary Disclaimer

The characters' names were changed to protect them, and in some cases, the stories are recollections of the way I remember them happening, which does not take away from their reality, but may differ from others' memories. Some of the details have been modified to preserve identifying details in some instances.

Preface

When a family lives in constant fear, each person in the household tends to be left with their own interpretation of what took place. Each experience that was felt, suffered, heard, and lived through has a different result and effect on each individual. For me, it began with my earliest memories from childhood and culminated with writing this memoir. Coincidence or not, it is the circle of my life. The stories told are from my current recollections. Some memories had been forgotten and returned to me only as I was writing. While the book is told from a third party point of view, this is also how I viewed myself—as being outside my body.

The life of a child is precious and requires nurturing—a lack of proper parenting results in a loveless, unvalidated life for the abused and the abuser. The main character, Patricia, spent more than half her life in therapy and never understood why she felt the way she did or why she fell prey to certain people. Her experiences included being trapped in a narcissistic, abusive romantic relationship and becoming a target for a narcissistic boss. By reading other people's stories and having "aha" moments, Patricia came upon her own realizations about her life and human connections. For many years she remained silent, not only about what she went through in each relationship but also the dysfunction she had suffered since birth. Growing up, she never thought of her parents as selfish, but the realization that they were gave Patricia freedom and relief from the guilt she had carried throughout her life.

This book is for the adult who was an abused and neglected child. Regardless of what one's family life dictates, everyone has the power to change their circumstances and become successful, productive individuals in society. We can also learn to break generational cycles of dysfunction and trauma to raise healthy adults. Knowledge is power, especially when it comes to matters of abuse, no matter what type of abuse you face. The more you know, the better you become at spotting perpetrators. If the situations in this book resonate, evaluate your past and current relationships. Get out of circumstances that are causing you harm. Do not stay silent; what you feel is real, valid, and must be heard.

The book uses humor to demonstrate certain situations. Humor is a survival tool often used to diminish the impact abuse leaves. In no way is it used to mock terror; humor is used to take away the power that terror can hold. And who doesn't like to laugh? Along with a vivid imagination, laughter helped Patricia survive. And in order to survive, you must use whatever weapons you have in your arsenal.

Prologue

"Is my baby alive?" asked the woman, exhausted from the labor. Three women from the maternity ward stood at the foot of the gurney, yelling at her to push.

"We've called for a doctor, and no one is coming. It looks like this baby is going to have to come out on its own," one of the women explained to the mother-to-be. Unable to hold the baby any longer, Maria gave one big push, and just as the baby was crowning, an intern and a nurse ran into the room. They assisted in the final minutes of the delivery. The newborn's body was limp, and her silence overtook the room.

"We are trying to get her to breathe," called out the intern. It was Holy Week in San Salvador, and all the doctors were on vacation. Maria had not attended one maternity checkup and found herself at the free clinic as the pain became unbearable. She could hear the interns talking amongst themselves.

"The baby seems to have drowned in the mother's womb. We are going to have to resuscitate her," said the nurse. Suddenly a cry emerges from the small body.

"Sounds of joy. One second more, and we would have lost the child," said the nurse.

CHAPTER 1

Crossing Borders

The screams on that hot Houston night were deafening as the woman called out for help.

"Stop hurting her," the young boy pleaded. His small body crashed into the furniture as he stood between his father and mother. Antonio was in a rage, completely incoherent, with a belt in his hand. The cracking sounds of the belt zoomed by his ears with every strike. The screams from Maria, not just Antonio's wife but also his prey, got louder as the welts on her body rose.

In the dark closet, birds chirped, the lake glistened from the sun's rays, children played ball, ran, and laughed. And Patricia, a timid five year old, uncurled her body as she held her breath, hoping the violence would come to an end. As her mind suddenly returned to the room and away from the fairyland of her imagination, her brother

Tony's limp body hit the bed, and Patricia's screams echoed into the void. There was no one to hear and no one to help.

The room with the bunk beds that Patricia and Tony shared was filled with toys and was now the scene of a horrific, violent attack. While other children had Sunday dinners and played board games with their parents, this was family night in the Lopez house.

Only this time, Antonio had gone too far. Maria was left bloody and unrecognizable, her face swollen, her eyes bruised and shut. Her body ached from the lashes of the belt, and she could barely move. In a daze, Maria mustered up every ounce of willpower to crawl through the darkness, feeling around the small mobile home. Reaching and grasping, she followed the sounds that came from her weeping children. She finally heard the door shut as Antonio left the house. She was relieved he was gone, but the pain was unbearable; her body throbbed as her mind raced. Soon, a feeling of despair overtook her mind, body, and soul.

Maria knew she had to flee. She needed to get out quickly. But with no family or friends nearby, she was at a loss as to what to do. She began walking and finally managed to bring herself to the doorstep of a kind acquaintance. She had once engaged in conversation with him at the local grocery store and hoped he would remember her. Taking one look at her, the man named Christopher went into quick action and called on his nephew to drive the woman and her two children back to their country, El Salvador. Just like that, Christopher put the three of them in a car. They had only the clothes they were wearing. No money, no personal belongings, nothing but each other. They drove 1,795 miles through three borders, numerous deserts, and gangs of Bandidos to reach their destination.

Maria was born into a formidably wealthy family who had immigrated from Jerusalem to El Salvador in the early 1900s. With short, curly, jet-black hair, a small stature, and a medium frame, she was the epitome of an attractive Middle Eastern woman. She began to work at the tender age of 16 in order to escape her abusive family. Constantly plagued with insecurity and feelings of worthlessness, her life was nothing short of perpetual chaos.

Her mother was an outcast for marrying outside the family lineage and then divorcing. Divorced and mentally ill with schizophrenia, Maria's mother took to living on the streets with her two children. On occasion, they would be taken in by Maria's grandparents.

Much to everyone's chagrin, Maria's dark features, high cheekbones, and defined jawline resembled those of her father, and her maternal grandparents could not bear to look at her. They treated her poorly, constantly degrading her. She struggled through a loveless childhood and jumped at the first chance of escape: Antonio. He was the first man, the first *person*, to show her any semblance of affection.

Tony was born when Maria was 18, and Patricia followed one year later. She had no skills to take care of herself, let alone two children. Antonio's ambitions were to go to the United States; he knew better opportunities were there. But he couldn't initially go with Maria and the children, so he settled in Texas and sent Maria money to rent a small house. Sometimes Maria and the children even lived with her mother and brother, Juan. On weekends, they would spend time with her grandparents in their palatial home. The children were surrounded by family, as dysfunctional as they could be.

When Tony was five years old and Patricia was four, Antonio sent word to Maria that the papers were in order for Maria to come to America with the children. With a heavy heart, Maria uprooted the children from the only home they had ever known and joined her husband in Houston. Antonio's affection soon turned into sadistic punishments and explosive rage episodes. As the abuse worsened, Maria was at a loss—fearful for her life and those of her children. One year later, under the cover of darkness, she fled with her children.

With nowhere else to go, Maria had no choice but to return to her grandparents' doorstep, just as her mother had done years before with her two children. She was bruised, battered, and defeated.

The stranger, who she learned during their trip was named Johnathan, drove them nonstop, occasionally pulling over for gas and food. Maria sat in the passenger's seat and would constantly turn back around to check on Tony and Patricia—at times fearful, at times talkative, and often asleep even as they crossed over bumpy terrain. With barely any money to her name, their future was uncertain. As they got further from Houston, Patricia and Tony worried about many things, but their main concern revolved around Santa Claus, since the next day was Christmas Eve. Would Santa be able to find them? Unable to understand what was happening as the landscape changed around them, they held onto each other. Patricia's thoughts raced back to the fallen Christmas tree in their living room, her toys left behind, and the bedroom she and Tony had shared. Was it gone forever?

When they finally arrived in San Salvador two days after leaving Houston, the children were greeted by their mother's brother, their Uncle Juan. *What a surprise!* A favorite of Patricia's, he was like a father to her, and being reunited with him was a gift. He held her tight and gave her a doll. Tony was given a toy airplane. Uncle Juan's arms enveloped her like a warm blanket.

"You are safe," he whispered in her ear. For the first time in what seemed like years, Patricia felt herself breathe.

Patricia was glad to be in a place where she was not afraid. Loving all the attention her great-grandfather Eli and Uncle Juan showered her with, she pinched herself to make sure it was not a dream. Despite the tension between her mother and her great-grandparents, Patricia felt free. There was no screaming, fighting, or hitting. Patricia and Tony had space to run and play and be children. Most importantly, they had peace and freedom.

The house was grand, with a luxurious courtyard surrounded by an expanse of rooms. Tucked away in one of those rooms was Patricia's grandmother. Maria's schizophrenic mother had a nervous breakdown, leading to her parents taking her back into their home. Grandma's room was dirty and smelled of old, wet, moldy paper. In the bathroom, she hoarded newspapers, which she used as toilet paper. Though the rest of the house was kept immaculate under the watchful eye of the housekeeping staff, they did not dare enter Grandma's room for fear of being accused of stealing from the old woman. Grandma's schizophrenia would get the best of her, and she frequently lashed out at the help.

Grandma loved to tell Patricia stories. All kinds of stories. Some true, some questionable. Patricia did not mind the overbearing smell of Grandma's room as long as she could hear the stories. Grandma's room was a menagerie, with a parrot who repeated everything it heard and a three-legged dog. These animals had become Grandma's only real companions, in addition to Patricia.

But Patricia's most cherished times were with Uncle Juan. He would play the guitar and sing for her every night. The music was joyful and uplifted her spirits. It was the happiest she had been in a long time. After decades, the house was filled with small children, their noise, fights, and energy. It was a new sensation for her great-grandparents and was not always well-received. Maria tried her best to contain the children, but they were rambunctious and needed to release their pent-up energy. Tony, in particular, was the greater troublemaker and would manage to get on the last nerves of all the elders in the home.

Patricia, however, was the apple of great-grandpa Eli's eye. She could do no wrong in his heart and head even when Patricia was the provocateur. One afternoon, Tony was chasing Patricia through the house, and Patricia was looking back at him, sticking her tongue out and teasing him. She turned her face just in time to plow into a cement pillar. Her front teeth lay in small pools of blood on the white marble floors as she was sprawled on her back, screaming from the pain. The entire household surrounded her within seconds, and they quickly rushed her to the hospital. It was a normal childhood accident, but Tony became persona non grata for Eli.

On another occasion, Patricia was skipping through the long corridor of the house, singing and dancing with her pigtails flying and white sneakers squeaking. Her foot landed in a bucket of red paint. Without stopping, she continued throughout the house, leaving red tracks with each step. Oblivious and unaware of where the destructive prints were coming from, a raging Eli followed the footprints up and down every hallway. Finally, he caught her by the arms and turned her around. Instead of anger, his face softened.

"There's my angel," he proclaimed, smiling. "If it would have been that devil Tony, I'd have taken a switch to him!" Eli said it loud enough so that Tony would hear, even though Tony was nowhere near the scene.

As great-grandpa Eli walked away and left Patricia to continue playing, she wondered, *How can he be so calm? Am I going to suffer the consequences?* Unsure and scared of what might happen next, she looked around for her mother and brother, worried he would lash out at them for what she had done. But the house was calm and quiet. At that moment, she realized forgiveness was possible. One did not need to live in constant fear.

Months went by. Maria's external wounds healed, and the children felt free. Then, one afternoon, Eli answered a knock at the door. It was Antonio. Patricia hid behind the bathroom door. She tried to hear what they were saying, but Patricia's father and great-grandfather were in a deep, huddled discussion. Finally, she could make out some of what they were saying. Texas was mentioned. Suddenly the discussion was over, and Eli called for everyone to gather in the corridor.

"Your father is here for you," Eli looked down at Patricia and forced a smile. Patricia could not believe what she was hearing. Surely this man who showed her love and kindness would not send her off. She knew Eli would not let her live in torment. It must be a mistake!

Maria would not look up at her grandfather's face. She knew that no matter what Antonio had done to her, no matter how much he violated her, Eli respected Antonio. Antonio was handsome, fit, had light brown hair and sparkly eyes with a hazel hue. He was raised in the countryside—penniless—in a small, thatched-roof house with dirt floors and eight brothers and sisters. His father was an extremely abusive machista who had no regard for his wife or children. Affection in Antonio's childhood home consisted of slaps and extreme punishments. Despite his lack of formal education, Antonio was pragmatic, intelligent, and self-sufficient. He always knew he would leave his small home for bigger things. At the age of 15, Antonio fled his abusive home and headed for the city. A wealthy businessman who owned an auto shop noticed him hanging around and took him under his guidance. Antonio was a quick learner and soon knew all aspects of the auto shop. During that time, he met Maria and decided she would be his wife. The children were born soon after. Eventually, the auto shop owner asked Antonio to run his business. With a wealth of automotive knowledge under his belt, Antonio migrated to the United States and built his career as a successful mechanic in Houston.

Eli admired Antonio for being a self-made success. Whatever the differences and disagreements between Antonio and Maria were, Eli was certain they could be worked out when the family was back in the United States. He was sure that Antonio was not an unreasonable man, and Maria and the children needed someone to care for them. Eli was too old to be able to provide for the young family, and he would not be around forever. He believed it was important for Maria to be with her husband and the children to be with their father and felt they should return home to Houston.

The next day Maria, Tony, and Patricia joined Antonio on a flight back to Houston. Maria once again felt that there was no one to trust. The plane ride was torture, knowing she was going back to a life of uncertainties, chaos, and terror. Maria did not speak. Tony and Patricia held their breath, waiting for some sort of reassurance to come out of their mother's mouth, telling them that everything would be okay. None did.

How could Maria reassure her children? She was unsure of what they were in for back in Houston. Maria wanted to make things different but did not know how. She thought of Johnathan, who had taken them across the country, and the risk he took to save them. It had all been for nothing.

CHAPTER 2

Looking for Friends

Things were quiet for a few days, the proverbial calm before the storm. But soon enough, with nowhere for Maria or the children to go, Antonio's abuse began again. They were living in their mobile home off Main Street, a quiet community of mostly retired couples. There were no children other than the resident manager's son, a 15 year old who suffered from social anxiety.

Maria was not well, silently suffering from depression. She spent hours in total darkness, lying in bed with a towel over her head. She claimed to have migraine headaches. Patricia would lay outside the bedroom door and hope her mother would get up. Patricia felt sad and insecure, her chest tight and her stomach queasy. She felt abandoned despite the fact that her mother was just on the other side of the door. All she wanted to do was go back to her great-grandfather's house. Things were better there; her mother even smiled there. Months went by, and Maria finally went to the doctor and was prescribed Valium. Unfortunately, the medication caused her to withdraw even further, shutting herself within her mind and leaving the children to fend for themselves.

Patricia's loneliness and anxiety grew. When she felt this way, she remembered the lake in San Salvador, the children playing, how great it was to be there, and her peace. Patricia decided that the lake was where she lived, not the mobile home in Houston. She didn't need an airplane to get there; it was all in her imagination, and she could get there anytime she wanted.

Though Maria had been in America for over a year, she had not yet learned to drive a car. Antonio was reluctant to teach her. It was one more way for him to control her and keep her within the walls of the house. Since the elementary school was one mile away, the children walked down busy Main Street each morning, holding hands and pretending that life was great. One day, they noticed two ladies on swings. It looked like great fun to be swinging all day long, sailing high above the ground. The women wore glittered bathing suits that didn't cover much. The ladies waved at the children as they passed by on their way to school. The building they hung outside had lots of bright neon, flashing lights, and a fence to keep unnecessary onlookers out. *It must be some sort of secret hideout*, the children thought. Patricia proclaimed that the women would be her new friends and decided she would bring snacks. After all, it had to be hard work swinging high above the buildings.

One day, on their way home after school, they walked by the brightly lit shop front and saw Antonio's car. So they attempted to go in and see what their dad was doing.

"This place is not for children," a large man at the entrance said as he stopped them. They ran home and told their mother what they had seen and experienced. When Antonio arrived home, Maria questioned him.

"Why were you in that strip bar? The children walked by and saw your car." Before she could continue, he slapped her and threw her to the ground.

"Don't you question me, woman!" he yelled.

"Give me my dinner," he demanded. "Your job is to have it ready." The children watched in fear. Patricia felt tremendously guilty. She should never have told her mother what they had seen. Then, as if nothing had happened, they all sat down to dinner.

Patricia was not adept at making friends. She had no sense of self-worth and didn't believe she had anything to offer other people. She often went to school with wrinkled clothes and tangled hair. It was hard for her to pay attention in school. Everything seemed irrelevant compared to what was happening at home. Patricia admired the other girls that wore cute dresses, patent leather shoes, and perfect pigtails. She looked and felt out of place. They all played outside in the court-yard at recess, turning flips on the monkey bars. Patricia would just watch from a distance. She felt invisible, often sitting alone at lunch. Every day her mother would make her lunch, and without fail, one of the girls in her class would take it and throw it in the garbage. Finally, tired of it, she went home and told Maria she wanted to buy her lunch instead. When Maria questioned her about it, Patricia had no choice but to finally tell her mother what had been happening at school. No matter her level of depression or the abuse she received, Maria was as ferocious as a lion when it came to anyone harming her children.

The following day Maria marched up to the school with Patricia.

"Point out who is doing this to you," she demanded. Patricia reluctantly pointed out one of the girls. The teacher stepped out of the classroom that morning, and the children were left without adult supervision. Maria charged at the child, grabbed her, threw her in a closet, and slammed the door.

"We will see if you throw any more lunches away!" The teacher walked in just at that moment.

"What's going on?" she asked.

"This girl takes Patricia's lunch and throws it in the garbage, and I will not tolerate it!" Maria raised her voice, accusing the teacher as much as the student.

"I will talk with the girls, but I think it's time for you to go home." The teacher was in shock, slightly humiliated, and also felt violated having a parent commandeer her classroom in such a way.

After that, Patricia continued to eat outside by herself. One of the other students saw her and asked if she could sit next to her. Patricia just stayed quiet. The girl's name was Denise.

"You don't look like you're from here," Denise said.

Patricia replied with a lie, "I'm from the Philippines."

Denise was impressed, "Is it far from here?"

Patricia would answer with more lies. She knew nothing about the Philippines or even where it was, but it sounded different. Lying would become her way of hiding the parts of herself that she did not want others to see.

Patricia found comfort in her lies. Like a drug addict seeking a high, she found relief from the stories she told. And, like an addict, her addiction was getting bigger and bigger. She went so far as to profess, "I'm changing my identity altogether." One day, during Show and Tell, she walked into class and told everyone she was a famous roller skater.

"It is hard work," she said, "and very hard practicing every day after school." To make the story more believable, she took one of Tony's trophies for the next Show and Tell. She would dream of skating, applause, and fame. The other kids loved the stories, and they started taking an interest in her.

Two days later, her mother came to school. The children asked if they could come to see Patricia skate. Maria looked at them and said, "She can't skate. She has two left feet." Maria was confused as she looked at the eager children. And just like that, it was the end of Patricia's childhood fame. Patricia was devastated. Her mother had ruined everything. Patricia's plan had failed but she was determined to find new stories to tell and new people to tell them to. She vowed to no longer merely be the class helper and refused to sit on the sidelines.

The most fun Patricia had was playing pretend with Tony outside their house. Patricia was always a singer, and Tony was a race car driver. The mobile home community management did not allow anyone to use the swing set on the property. However, Tony was cunning and figured they would wait until sunset when the management office was closed for the day and then they could swing to their hearts desire. It went on almost every night.

Then Tony enrolled in karate lessons. Patricia was not allowed to because she was a girl. "Girls don't do karate," professed Antonio. One afternoon when Tony was gone, Patricia walked to the swing set, and the manager's son was there. She had seen him lurking around before, but he always ran off as Tony and Patricia were together. This time, seeing that Patricia was alone, he approached her. The manager's son asked if she lived in the blue and white house. Patricia didn't answer but the boy acted nervous. He asked his question and had no other words to say. Patricia stared at him. His eyes were empty, his skin pale, and his greasy hair fell below his eyebrows, leaving just enough room for her to see their intensity. Suddenly he grabbed her and dragged her through the alley. She felt his sweaty fingers around her arm as he took her behind the house. He put his hand over her mouth and told her not to scream. She closed her eyes and imagined the lake, the children, and the peace. She focused on her thoughts and imagined her mother coming to look for her. She could feel his warm breath close to her face, his hand grasping at her.

"Don't scream, don't scream," he kept repeating the words over and over.

The sun was starting to set as it was getting darker. She could smell the night air. *It's dinner time*, she thought. Suddenly, she heard her mother calling out her name, "Patricia, Patricia!" The boy panicked, looked around, and ran off. Maria came around the corner of the alley.

"What are you doing back here? Dinner is ready." Patricia did not answer. *She won't understand.*

Guilt took over. *What did I do wrong?* Scared, she decided then and there that she would not say a word. She had so many secrets. What was one more? In her mind, she questioned the events that had just occurred. *Did I make that happen? Is there some way I connected with my mother by having her come right away? Did I bring her to my rescue? Something I have been incapable of doing for her?* Patricia paused, lept up, and hugged her mother. She hugged her so tight that she could not breathe. Maria looked at her and asked if she was ok.

"You seem startled," Maria said, "and you're all dirty." Unsure of what to say, Patricia asked if Tony was back from his karate lesson. "Yes," replied her mother.

"I want to take karate," she demanded. "I want to go with Tony. Please, mom, convince dad to let me go." She did not know what Maria did or said, but the following week Patricia took her first karate lesson.

Patricia was ready. She wanted to learn to defend herself. Tired of all the uncertainties coming at her, it was imperative to fight back. Even at a young age, she had witnessed too many battles lost by victims who gave up. She was not going to give up. She was determined to protect herself and thus began her mission.

CHAPTER 3

Sink or Swim

Patricia wasn't the only one who needed defending. Maria lived in constant fear, not knowing what to expect on any given day. Antonio's auto repair shop was close to their house. He would return home late most nights, claiming to be working until then and expected a warm dinner to be waiting for him upon arrival. It was a crapshoot when he would arrive, and no one else was allowed to eat until he was home. To keep the peace, they all reluctantly conformed. Family dinners were like Russian roulette. They never knew which Antonio they were going to get. On some nights, if he didn't like the food, he'd go into a rage and throw his plate against the wall. Then there were the nights when he was in a good mood; he had satisfied his needs before arriving home and was tolerable. Regardless, everyone stuck to the script as if they were actors in a play.

Maria worked hard. She cooked and cleaned profusely, obsessively, as if she was trying to wipe all the chaos away. Sometimes she would go over things two or three times a day. Unfortunately, her cleaning was never enough. She made Patricia clean the bathroom that she and Tony shared, vacuum the carpet, and wipe the windows. It was never good enough. "Fold the towels," she said. Patricia would fold the towels. "That's not how you do it!" she would shout and then throw the towels on the floor. "Redo it." There was no pleasing her. Her actions and words towards the children were the only things Maria could control. For Patricia, life consisted of fear, uncontrollable outbursts, and demands from her parents. There was nothing carefree or childlike about her childhood. Most times, she dreamt of running away. Any place had to be better than this.

Children's activities were seldom on the Lopez family agenda, but weekends consisted of day-long soccer games for Antonio. Patricia's father was part of a league and aspired to be a kicker in the NFL. He tried out for the Houston Oilers and was cut in the last round of try-outs. He then decided to enlist in the Army after learning they had a football team. He had to pass an English proficiency exam in reading and writing as part of the process. With no formal education, he failed the test and was rejected from the Army. Before it was all over, Antonio was profiled in the local newspaper as a dedicated immigrant, willing to give his life to serve the country where he now lived. The article portrayed him as an outstanding citizen, but nowhere in it did it mention his true personality or the family dynamics he was a part of; it failed to say he was an abusive husband or father.

Rejection from the NFL nor the Army dissuaded him from following his passion. He would force the entire family to watch him play soccer from sun up to sun down each weekend. They saw the same people week in and week out. Some were nice and some not so nice. Most of the time, they were rather pathetic. The environment could get ugly, more like a prison yard than a wholesome family playground. Players would sit around drinking beer all day, before and after the games, and often relieve themselves on the side of the bleachers. It was not an environment for children.

One afternoon, soccer finished earlier than usual, and the Lopez clan was invited to the home of one of the other players and his wife. They were promised a barbeque and a swim. The children were thrilled and hoped that Antonio would accept the invitation. He usually abstained from taking Maria and the kids anywhere, let alone spending time with other people. But, to everyone's surprise, Antonio gladly said they would all go. As they arrived at the couple's house, Antonio grabbed Maria's arm and pushed her against the car.

"Listen to me," he said, pointing his fist at her face. "Keep to yourself and don't make conversation." Maria just nodded; she knew she was always meant to be silent and hidden. Patricia and Tony ran off to jump in the pool; they knew their father's treatment would be bestowed upon their mother. But that day, they were at a new house, and there was a pool that needed to be jumped in!

The apartment complex was small and quaint, with the pool as the centerpiece surrounded by lush gardens. They ran from the chaos into paradise, following the smell of burning charcoal from the grill, as the sun's rays warmed their backs.

The hosts were already in the pool laughing and joking. They were a young couple from Costa Rica without children. They had asked to babysit Patricia and Tony many times, but Antonio always denied their request. Marco, the husband, was interested in mechanics and had taken a liking to Antonio. He looked up to Antonio as if he had achieved a lot in a short time. His wife was still trying to acclimate to a different country and had found comfort in talking to Maria.

Suddenly, being young and carefree, Marco took his wife and turned her upside down, dunking her. Tony and Patricia were on the shallow end of the pool. As the screams reached them, Patricia looked up and reacted with fear. Something looked wrong to her, and she was overcome with a sense of urgency to take immediate action. She dove into the deep end, putting aside the fact that she could not swim. Imagining herself to be a superhero, she leaped into the air and landed in the water. But instead of swimming, her body sank.

Further and further, she went into the depths, unable to control her body. Finally, her head hit the bottom of the pool. She could see the rays of light as they poked through. She heard the children playing ball, running, laughing, and the birds chirping as she slowly drifted away. Then, out of nowhere, Antonio jumped into the pool, clothes and all. To the rescue!

Patricia opened her eyes, coughing and spitting water as she slowly regained consciousness. She was confused and immediately asked if the hostess was okay.

"What were you thinking? Are you stupid?" Antonio was dripping wet and yelling at her. At that moment, she wished she had stayed at the bottom of the pool. It could have been more peaceful. At no point would Antonio have considered the fact that had he been watching his children instead of yelling at their mother, none of this would have happened.

After Patricia's near-drowning, Antonio sentenced her to be confined to the house with her mother—no friends nor social activities. "This is best for everyone," said Maria meekly. In reality, Maria wanted Patricia with her for selfish reasons. Unable to make friends and with no one else to talk to, Patricia's presence gave Maria a sense of being a little less alone. Unable to understand why life was so restricted, Patricia became extremely resentful. *Tony gets to be outside. He doesn't have to abide by dumb rules. He doesn't have to stay in and keep mom company.* In their household, there were two sets of rules, one for boys and one for girls. Patricia was to act like a young lady and learn domestic chores. Tony was supposed to learn to be tough, to be the hunter-gatherer. Patricia was bored to death of cleaning the house and watching television while her brother and all the neighborhood kids were outside riding bikes and having fun.

When Tony would come back home after a day of adventures, he would drone on about all the games he had played and places he had explored with his friends on their bikes. Tony had far more freedom than Patricia, but things were not particularly rosy for him either. Tormented by his home life, he struggled with his identity and was constantly bullied and forced into fights.

Tony's childhood responsibilities weighed down on him. From a young age, he carried the burden of protecting his mother and sister while also being tortured by his father. Antonio continuously drilled into him that he needed to "be a man." But what he truly needed was the love that a father gives a young boy. It would be too much for anyone to bear, let alone a young child. Tony found his coping mechanism in food. Though he was overweight, he was active—a handsome young man with jet black hair and chiseled features.

Tony and Patricia were constantly at each other's throats, so much so that Maria always had to separate them. When it became too much for Maria to bear, she disciplined them severely. She punished them the only way she knew how; the way she had been punished as a child. One favorite form of torment was putting salt on their backs and forcing them to lick it off each other. Maria would walk over to the pantry, take out the canister of Morton's salt, and as if she were seasoning a roast, she would sprinkle it on their backs. As sprinkles of salt hit Patricia's back, she'd become tense and swallow her tears. Tony's back would glisten from sweat as the grains of salt would stick.

If her mother heard her cry, Patricia knew the punishment would be worse.

Patricia always had to go first. She'd closed her eyes tight, but as she got close to Tony, the smell of sweat and salt was overbearing, and she dropped to her knees, pleading for forgiveness. Then, there would be total silence. Eventually, Maria would break and send them to their room.

Maria yelled constantly at them. It was her way of communicating. She did not know how to speak or garner respect unless it was with aggression. And she threw things. Any object lying still could be turned into a projectile missile. Toys and shoes were constantly launched at Tony and Patricia. It would turn into a game of dodgeball, except the children were dodging household items instead of a soft, rubber ball. Once, failing to duck in time, Tony was branded with "GAP" on his back from the underside of a flying shoe. After that, Maria merely had to look at the children with her hard eyes, and they would quickly stand at attention.

With Antonio rarely at home, both caretaking and disciplinary duties fell on Maria. She was constantly suspicious of his whereabouts and activities but feared that even questioning him would bring about levels of retaliation that Maria dared not imagine. It was not unusual for him to come home with makeup on his white t-shirt and simply toss it in the laundry with the rest of his clothes for Maria to wash. Maria would find them, carry the shirts over to the window, fling the curtains open and hold them to the light as she'd call Patricia over. Maria would fume, "Look at this? Do you see this? He claims to be working late." Patricia would just stare. Maria would smell the clothes, "Perfume. This is not mine." Patricia would think to herself, *Wouldn't it be better if he left with another family?* But she never said these things out loud.

Not knowing where to turn and feeling completely isolated, Maria decided to hire a private investigator. The detective took pictures of Antonio with several different women in various situations. In some scenarios, he was the one pursuing the women. These pictures showed him sitting at dinner, going to the movies, and enjoying drinks. It was as if he was happily coupled off—except each image was with a different woman. Then there were the ones of him being conquered. Many women found him alluring, propositioned him, and paid for his time. Antonio would park his car down the street from their homes, be in and out within a few hours, and always during the middle of the day. These women were much older and very wealthy. He had met most of these women when they had come into his shop to have their vehicles repaired.

Maria had the proof she needed and finally mustered up the courage to confront her cheating, lying husband. Antonio denied everything. Even with photographic evidence against him, he accused Maria of being crazy. With each photo, he denied more and more.

"I don't know anything about what you're saying. You're a crazy, stupid person, and if you don't stop, I'm going to leave you on the streets." Holding punishments over her head for her accusations always worked. Maria was afraid and did not dare take action.

Maria was beyond indignant and also desperate. There was no one to believe her. One night, after hanging up the phone with the detective and sobbing uncontrollably, she took the envelope to Maria and Tony and showed the children what their father was doing. "Unbelievable!" She kept repeating as she told them how he spent his time away from his family and how he received money from women for non-mechanical work. She was a woman who was unraveling and could not rationalize that sharing this information with her young children would cause them long-term harm. Even more unbelievable than the pictures themselves was the fact that her impressionable children were now holding them in their small hands. Intimate details of a marriage that should have remained between Maria and Antonio were now being told to Tony and Patricia as if they were a bedtime story. But without anyone to listen to her, Maria's only audience was her children. She needed validation for her suffering and Antonio's actions.

What was a child to say or do? Patricia went to her room and started writing. Her eyes became heavy; tears poured out as she sat at her desk. So many emotions surfaced, her arms tingled with energy, and without thinking, the pen took over into poems and stories, all with fatal and sorrowful outcomes, coming from her hand, through the pen, and onto the paper. The words were just flowing from her. Suddenly it stopped, and so did the tingling. The heavy weight on her had diminished. She no longer felt scared or confused, though quite the opposite. It felt good to leave the feelings there, close the book, and carry on. Patricia looked around. She was alone in the room but felt that someone was with her. Writing her thoughts down was an out-of-body experience, as if she was not the one writing but instead was someone who was watching over her. Patricia was grateful for whatever it was. She liked to think of it as her guardian angel relieving her of overwhelming pain.

Patricia began to write with greater frequency. Then, one day, she drew a picture instead of writing. The drawing was of a black house with one window and a high picket fence around it. She had drawn different versions of this house previously, but this time it was black. The picture triggered confusion in Patricia. It seemed dark and scary and she wanted to discuss it with Maria. She handed the drawing to her mother but Maria barely looked at it and put it away without saying a word.

"Can we talk about it?" Patricia quietly asked. Maria looked down at her and replied, "Not now." Maria barely even looked at what Patricia was anxiously holding out for her. In reality, Maria was consumed only by her inner torment, her depression, and her lack of a life. Most days, she walked around hypnotic and in a daze. Patricia had no understanding of this. She could see that nothing she did could make her mother happy. This frustrated Patrica as Tony received much praise for everything he did. In Patricia's eyes, Tony made his mother happy, but perception is not always realistic. All Patricia knew was that Tony was always favored over her. Even though Patricia tried, she would never be seen and would remain invisible.

Antonio belittled Tony every chance he got. He called him names and told him he was fat, would never amount to anything, and yelled at him to find a woman and stop watching television. At seven years old, Tony had no clue what his father was yelling at him about, but the words echoed for him the rest of his childhood. This depressed Maria even more. As strict as she was with both of the children, seeing Tony degraded by his father made her want to offset some of that abuse by paying extra attention to her son and praising him whenever possible.

Patricia's nights were filled with restless sleep, and she always woke up exhausted. Nightmares ruled her night, waking up at midnight in a cold sweat. Barely drifting off to sleep, she would sense her door open. She would see a shadow and a hand. Then she would feel like a heavy weight was upon her small body. Suddenly, her mind would drift off. Patricia would imagine being at her lake with a loving soul, the one that would take care of her. It was a rollercoaster of emotions. The dreams always ended the same way, leaving her feeling fearful and confused. Her room was right next to Tony's. In the mornings after those dreams, she would ask him if he heard anything. He always replied with a "no."

She did not know what was worse: not knowing what the nightmares were about or being confused between a horrendous dream and reality. If it was a nightmare, she needed to learn how to erase it and make it go away. Before going to bed, she would try to recall all the beautiful scenes that drifted through her mind. Calmness would take over as she drifted to sleep, but the frightening dreams did not stop.

BEAUTIFUL MIND

The mind is a beautiful thing protecting us from the past

Holding back deep dark fragments

Never allowing us to fray

If you ask, it answers

If you seek, it reveals

Like a movie playing out

It often leaves us wondering

Pondering for the truth within us, embrace it

The truth flows through our being

It's our creator

It lives within us

It runs through our veins

Carries our laughter and our pains

Accept its existence and relinquish its internal stain

CHAPTER 4

Can Anyone Hear Me?

Her eighth birthday was quickly approaching, and Patricia was getting excited. Her birthday always came during the Easter holidays and with it, springtime.

She laid outside on the grass, feeling the warmth of the sun, the breeze of the wind, the smell of the flowers blooming. *It is a new beginning*, she thought. She closed her eyes and imagined leaving. She would fly away and go to other lands and visit other families. She felt happy and safe. There was always someone with her on her journeys; she could feel their presence next to her. It was the same presence that was with her when she wrote. In her daydreams, she was in control. She could go wherever she desired and see anyone she wanted. The world was so bright. She envisioned herself as an adult, living a happy and healthy life.

Maria baked Patricia a cake and invited some neighborhood children to celebrate and sing. They were mainly Tony's friends. It was a small party, but Patricia was delighted. Unfortunately, Antonio soon forgot the reason for the celebration. He decided to invite his friends to the house to grill and have beers. As the kids played, the men became rowdy. The night ended with Antonio yelling at everyone and stumbling drunk to bed. And with Patricia in tears.

Patricia was becoming more of a recluse, keeping to herself and making herself invisible. But in the third grade, her teacher, Ms. Kasner, finally took notice. A newlywed, Ms. Kasner had shoulder-length, light brown hair with streaks of gray. Tall and slender, she would stand in front of the classroom and make it a point to call on the children who did not raise their hands. Ms. Kasner was strict but kind. She got Patricia more involved in the classroom, encouraging her to read and develop her writing skills. The teacher had become enamored by Patricia's kindness and timid disposition. The adult's attention instilled confidence in the impressionable child.

Among Patricia's classmates was a boy named Jacob. Jacob had dirty blonde hair, was skinny as a rail, had freckles, and wore the same shirt almost every day. Patricia developed a crush on him. She wracked her brain thinking of ways to capture his attention. Soon, she started to take more interest in herself, dressing nicer and brushing her hair. Patricia daydreamed of Jacob kissing her, just like the prince always kissed the princess in the books she read.

The children were seated in alphabetical order, which meant Patricia sat next to Grey, a young boy with a learning disability. She would help him with his assignments and try to be a good classmate. He was short-tempered and would throw fits. During one of these moments, he threw an Elmer's glue bottle at the teacher. That was the last day

Grey was in class; he was assigned to a different classroom after that incident. It also meant that Patricia would get a new seatmate: Jacob. She felt sorry for Grey but could not be happier with the new seating arrangement. Jacob and Patricia became friends. They would eat lunch together in the cafeteria and play on the playground. The two were cute together, and Ms. Kasner took notice.

Over the December break, Ms. Kasner invited the third-grade class to her house with their families. Patricia was nervous at the prospect of going with her parents, but she wanted to go. Finally, she convinced her mother and father to take her. They obliged, not wanting to leave a bad impression on the teacher. Ms. Kasner had made traditional Jewish foods for the holidays, wanting to expose the children to different cultures. During the evening, Ms. Kasner commented on how Patricia and Jacob's friendship had grown and how wonderful it was to see. Antonio overheard, silently looked at Maria, and continued with the evening as if everything was fine. But that night, Maria went to bed with cuts and bruises on her arms and legs.

"This should teach you a lesson. Keep your daughter under control. I hope this serves as a reminder of what is to come if she remains in that class." Antonio looked pathetically at Maria as he left the room.

The next day, Maria went to the school and demanded that Patricia be transferred to another class.

Ripped from her class and friends, Patricia was devastated. She felt there was no hope for her in any aspect of her life—not at home and not at school. After school that day, Patricia sat crossed-legged on her bed and wept. The tears came from a place deep inside her, her entire body shaking. She asked the universe for help and the stars for support. She asked anyone or anything out there to make things better.

"Can anyone hear me?" As the sadness overcame her, she felt a hand gently touch her shoulder. She quickly looked around. No one was there. At the same time, she heard a voice. A voice so clear it sounded as if it were coming from right next to her.

"Help yourself, and I will help you. You are strong. Lead the way." It was the softest, sweetest voice Patricia had ever heard. And as quickly as it had arrived, the presence she felt was gone. Patricia was startled but also felt peace. She wondered what the words meant. *Who is going to help me? What do they expect me to do? How can I control what is happening?* She recalled hearing those words from her great-grandfather on occasion. It was puzzling, but regardless, she decided not to overthink it; instead, she enjoyed the calmness it had left within her. She began looking forward to the spiritual visits; it was the one constant that was there for her in times of trouble.

A couple of days after the incident, Maria sat Patricia and Tony down. Patricia was so excited, thinking her mother would reveal a plan for freedom so that the three of them could escape and live a peaceful life. But to her and Tony's surprise, the news was that she was expecting a child. They were going to have a new brother or sister. And six months later, baby Elizabeth was born—the third victim to come into the Lopez household, an innocent child that would enter a world of darkness. Patricia was angry. She did not like this creature that had arrived. She tried her damndest to do everything in her power to make this new arrival leave, but that was not going to happen. Tony, on the other hand, had no reaction. *Dodging dad's insults should be easier now that he is distracted*, he thought. Despite his disinterest, protecting Elizabeth would be a priority. He felt responsible for the safety of the women in his life, and now he had one more to protect.

When Antonio first heard of the pregnancy, he was furious. He stayed out even later and was even more distant from Maria and the children. But when Elizabeth arrived, Pops (they had started calling him Pops after they watched the TV show *The Rifleman*) puffed his chest out to say, "That's my baby girl!" Somewhere along the way, he had changed his mind.

Elizabeth was the perfect baby; she was beautiful and healthy. Patricia oozed with jealousy. However, baby bottles accidentally broke, and Elizabeth accidentally rolled off the bed. *There are too many accidents to ignore*, thought Maria. Maria and Antonio sat down with Patricia and explained that she needed to show the baby kindness.

"No one loves me," Patricia burst into tears. "You love Tony more than me, and Pops is going to love the new baby more."

"This is not true. We all love you," Maria was trying to be gentle with Patricia. Love was not a word commonly used in the Lopez household. It seemed strange to hear. Patricia realized at that moment that her innocent sister was not to blame for her sorrow. It was a hell-hole long before Elizabeth arrived. If anything, Patricia should feel sorry for the baby—she had no clue about the insanity that awaited her.

Patricia began to question why God would send an innocent child to this house. Why would He want to punish her?

LOOK AT ME, HOLD MY GAZE

I can't see your face

Look past the dark

Drown the noise with my voice

I want to go to the dark

Feel me, sense me

Look in the mirror

See me

You are me, and I am you

Follow me, sit under the tree

Feel the ground, hear the sound

The sense of peace is profound

Here we renounce the pain

CHAPTER 5

Fighting Like Dogs and Goats

Out of nowhere, Antonio suddenly decided the family would move outside of the city. He got no objections from Maria or the children; everyone thought a change would be good. However, they were unaware that Antonio had an agenda. He wanted the family far away so he could continue doing as he pleased. He told them it was an excellent investment in an up-and-coming neighborhood. Little did they know what would await them.

The house Antonio had moved the family to was secluded. It was a new development with parks and open space. It was much bigger than the mobile home. With the arrival of Elizabeth, the space was welcome and needed. There was a backyard, and everyone would have their own room. The house was at the end of a dead-end road, overlooking a field full of cows and had ditches dotted with blackberry bushes. Tony was happy that the neighbors to the left had two boys his age, and some other kids in the neighborhood were similar in age.

As part of the move, Antonio promised the children they would get a dog. After all, they now had a backyard. Antonio had a client who bred German Shepherds. He took Tony and Patricia to his client's house and told them to choose one. They did not realize that these were not puppies but full-grown, ferocious beasts. They barked and snarled at them. It was like a scene from a horror movie or cop show. Reluctantly, they picked one of the pups and brought him home. They named him Ralph, the sound of the name was similar to the sound that came from his mouth when he barked. Ralph would dig holes and escape from the confines of the backyard. He scared the neighbors and destroyed their gardens, chased their cats, and caused havoc all around.

Ralph would accompany Antonio to the auto shop Monday through Friday. Antonio had no intention of giving the children a family pet; he merely wanted a guard dog. The children saw the dog on weekends when he was kept outside. They dared not go near him, he was vicious, and they feared he would attack any one of them.

A five-year-old little girl named Suzy lived in the neighborhood and would occasionally come to play with Elizabeth, who was now three. She was a spunky little thing with a cherub face and blonde hair. She took gymnastics lessons and was constantly doing cartwheels. One afternoon, she knocked on the door, but no one answered. So she went around back and opened the latch to the backdoor. Just as she closed the gate behind her, Ralph jumped on her little body. Patricia and Tony heard screaming. When they ran outside, they saw Suzy's limp body on the grass, covered in blood. Tony threw a rock at Ralph. It was the only way to get him away. The children cried for their mother to hurry up and come outside. When Maria saw the scene, she was in shock and mortified. Suzy was alive but in shock. Maria had no clue how somebody could ever explain this to her parents. She gathered the little girl in her arms and walked to her home. When they stood before her in shocked horror at the sight of their child, Maria explained to Suzy's parents that a dog had attacked the little girl, and then she practically fled from their doorstep, with Patricia and Tony following behind her. Suzy's parents quickly took the child to the emergency room. They were not going to question what happened—they had seen Antonio and had heard about his behavior; they had no desire to deal with him.

When they got home, Maria called Antonio to tell him what had happened. She pleaded with him to come home as soon as possible, but Antonio didn't seem to care about the accident and what had happened to Suzy. He came home well after midnight and went straight to bed, just like any other night.

The following day, Maria demanded that Antonio take the dog away and never bring him back. She didn't care what he did with the dog, as long as it was never near the house or the children again.

"You are always blowing everything out of the water; you're crazy and love to complain about everything. You hate the dog because he likes me." Antonio's reaction came as no surprise to anyone.

Maria's only response was, "Y'all are similar—vicious and un-controllable."

Suzy came back from the hospital with stitches along half of her doll-like face. Her parents forbid her to go near the house and play with the Lopez children ever again. They feared Antonio so much that they never confronted the family or took any action against them.

Ralph remained at Antonio's shop as a watchdog. They never mentioned the attack again but the sights and sounds of that after-noon stayed burned in the minds of Patricia and Tony for a long time. Antonio went about his business as if nothing had happened.

Sometimes Antonio had clients who couldn't always pay the bill. So he would connivingly hold their title or trade over them in those cases. One of his clients, who owned a farm, couldn't pay with money for a car repair, so he gave Antonio a goat. The goat remained in the shop for a few days. Antonio had no clue what he was going to do with a goat and then finally decided to bring it home in the middle of the night, unbeknownst to anyone else in the house. Elizabeth was the first to discover the goat. She looked out the glass door and started talking about the goat being outside. Maria, Tony, and Patricia had no clue what little Elizabeth was babbling about until they joined her at the door and saw—just as she said—there was a goat! Patricia took an immediate liking to the goat. Unlike the "guard" dog, this animal was docile and tame. He became her friend. She named him Dan.

A couple of months after Dan's unexpected arrival, Antonio decided to have a big barbeque at the house. He invited his friends from his soccer team, everyone who worked with him at the shop, and even random strangers he just happened to come across. Maria cooked all day and prepared food for grilling. Everyone was excited for a day of fun and freedom.

While playing outside, Patricia spied Antonio taking the goat around to the side of the house.

"Where are you taking Dan?" she innocently asked.

"He is the guest of honor," was Antonio's cool response. *What does that mean?*, thought Patricia. Shortly after, she heard a bleating sound and then silence. Antonio came around the corner, grinning ear to ear with pride, blood dripping from his hands. Patricia's heart sank, her body trembled, and tears rolled down her face as she froze in place.

Antonio walked past her in what seemed to be slow motion without even noticing Patricia. Dan's limp body in one hand and the machete he had used to butcher Dan in the other. She didn't want to believe her eyes, but poor Dan was the main entrée.

Patricia ran inside to look for comfort. There could be no crueler moment. Her father had demeaned and hurt her family before, but he had gone too far, taking the life of what she considered to be a family member. If only she could have said goodbye, but now she would never see him again.

Patricia looked around for her mother, looking for comfort, but Maria was caught up in an argument with Antonio. Patricia walked over, grabbing her hand. "Can't you see I'm busy?" Maria abruptly replied.

Jack, one of Antonio's soccer friends, walked over to her. "I'm so sorry," he said, "I can see the pain that caused you." Patricia just looked up at him as he put his heavy hand delicately on her shoulder. She didn't know how to process the violent act she knew had just happened. But in that moment, Jack was a comfort to Patricia. He had seen the events with the goat unfold.

Jack was a tall, burly British man with tattoos who owned a local pub; Uncle Jack, the children called him. Antonio and Jack played soccer together, and he was one of the only friends Antonio had that Patricia liked. Jack's voice was deep and commanding, and he could be intimidating, but not today.

Antonio had a soccer game the next day, and everyone had to go. But Maria stayed behind with Elizabeth, who wasn't feeling well. Patricia had another sleepless night; the recurring nightmare of someone coming into her room and bearing their weight on her had crept into her mind once more. She was exhausted and still dealing with the fact that Dan had been there one day and was gone the next, unable to process how no one said a word.

After the game, Antonio took the kids to Jack's pub. It was Sunday, and beers were half price. Patricia and Tony sat at the bar while Pops drank beer after beer. Patricia looked around and noticed that they were the only children.

Uncle Jack came by and said, "If anyone comes in and they look like a bobby," a slang term Patricia learned meant a British cop, "you need to run upstairs to my place." *If only a bobby would come by*, she thought.

Both kids were exhausted and would eventually fall asleep at the bar. Hours went by before Antonio finally put them in the car. Then he got behind the wheel, weaving the car as he drove. How he never got pulled over was always a mystery. It was bad enough that he took the kids in the car with him when he was drunk, but Antonio also drove with a tallboy in the seat next to him—so he wouldn't get thirsty on the drive home.

When they arrived at the house, Maria was awake waiting for them, worried that something had happened. Clearly, Antonio should not have been driving drunk with the kids in the car, but her fear of him striking her was so great that she didn't even bother questioning him.

"They have school tomorrow. You should have brought them home sooner," was Maria's cold statement.

"Shut up! You don't tell me what to do with my kids."

And with that, they all went to bed.

CHAPTER 6

Roller Coaster Rides

Time went on. Months felt like years and years like decades. Patricia was getting ready to start middle school; Tony had started there the previous year. He had made many friends and been selected for the school football team. To cope with his lack of confidence and questioning identity, Tony resorted to comedy. He had become the class clown; he would pull pranks and disrupt his classes. The teachers were constantly calling Maria to discuss his behavior. As much as she tried to instill discipline in him, it fell on deaf ears. Being popular made him feel alive, and after all, there was nothing wrong with making people laugh. It kept the bullies away and distracted him from his family life.

The first day of school was the worst. The school bus was full; there was not an empty spot to be found. Patricia had to sit next to a boy who smelled like smoke. She looked down at him as he was sitting in the aisle. His jeans were dirty and his white t-shirt wrinkled.

"Can you move over?" Her words were barely audible as she looked at the only open space next to him. He did not move, nor did he look up at her, so she squeezed by. She stared out the window and felt the tears welling up in her eyes. Her stomach tightened into knots as they got closer to the school. She felt ugly and inhuman. Even after moving houses, Patricia remained at the same elementary school on Main Street. She liked seeing the same faces every school year. Even though she felt like part of the furniture there, there was comfort in having consistency. Patricia had mastered disappearing. People had walked by her every day and never noticed her, and she was fine with that. She welcomed it. Now she would have to start over, and with zero social skills, it felt like an impossibility.

Lunch on the first day was a bewildering experience. Patricia entered the cafeteria and did everything in her power to make herself fade into the walls. She kept her head down and didn't look up to make eye contact with anyone. In trying to avoid everyone, she managed to walk right into a gathering of the most popular girls in school. They were smoking, wearing lots of makeup, and gossiping.

Consumed in conversation at first, they did not notice her. Patricia was relieved and figured she could quickly make an escape anywhere else. Then, out of nowhere, one of them looked over at her and asked for her name. Patricia looked around, not sure who they were talking to at first.

"You," one girl said, "I'm talking to you."

Patricia meekly gave them her name.

"Come sit with us." Their conversations revolved around the boys they had sex with over the summer and how many cigarettes they had smoked. Patricia remained mute. She had spent the entire summer locked up in the house with her mother. What could she possibly contribute to their conversation? When the bell rang announcing the end of the lunch period, the other girls scooted off and Patricia overheard them say, "There must be something wrong with her!" Maybe there *was* something wrong with her. She felt like an outcast. The only person she knew was Tony, and he was too busy with his friends. Patricia got through the day without speaking to anyone.

At home, the situation was getting worse by the day. Shortly after Elizabeth was born, the physical abuse stopped. Maria had managed to get a court order against him. That, however, did not stop the verbal abuse. It was more vicious than ever. Antonio would start drinking at work, drive home drunk, and be ready to fight by the time he arrived at the house.

Patricia would stay locked up in her room, but the constant yelling was ever-present and followed her no matter where she was. Elizabeth would cry from the noise, and Patricia did everything to comfort her. Her initial jealousy had turned into a need to protect the smallest member of their clan.

Maria could not take the abuse any longer and decided she needed a job. Saving money for a divorce would be the only way she could get out of the situation. Having no experience or any professional skills, the only jobs Maria could find were low-paying and at night. She arranged for Elizabeth to be looked after by a neighbor while she was away; Tony and Patricia were old enough to look after themselves. But Antonio would need to get them their dinner. The older children would wait for him, never knowing when he would show up and when they would get to eat. When Antonio finally arrived, stinking of alcohol and motor oil, he would put them in the car and drive them to a café for dinner. He flirted with the waitresses while the children ate, often falling over and making a spectacle of himself. Patricia and Tony ate in embarrassed silence.

Patricia dreaded the roller coaster rides in the car and humiliating moments at the restaurant, so she learned to cook. She would make meals for herself and Tony. They were slowly beginning to feel even more disconnected from their father and were developing their own methods of independence. Eventually, Maria saved enough money to hire a divorce lawyer.

"This is it! He is leaving this house!" Maria triumphantly declared. But Antonio never truly left. He might have disappeared for a few days, but he would always come back. Like a boomerang, they could never get rid of him.

One day, the bus ride to school wasn't as bad as usual. There was a girl sitting in the seat in front of Patricia. She looked back and smiled at her. Patricia had noticed the girl many times before. Her name was Becky. She was easy to spot, with black painted fingernails and always wearing the same white button-down shirt. Becky seemed to keep to herself, but came across as sassy; a bit of a rebel. Patricia coyly looked up to meet Becky's smile. They soon started chatting, and before long, they were hanging out in the local park, talking about how cool they would be in the seventh grade. Patricia would even spend time at Becky's house but would make sure to be home before Antonio got home—or else there would be hell to pay.

Seventh grade started, and with Antonio being away from them more and more, Patricia felt free to venture out and make more friends. After school one day, one of the boys asked if she wanted a ride home from school. She thought about it and reluctantly accepted the ride. As luck (or *un*luck) would have it, Antonio drove up to the house just as Patricia got out of her friend's car. He stared at her, saying nothing. She was scared, not sure what to expect. Patricia ran inside, up the stairs, into her room, and closed the door behind her. Minutes later, she heard yelling. Maria and Antonio were fighting, and the guilt overwhelmed Patricia. *It is all my fault. Why did I have to accept the ride?* Patricia walked downstairs, ready to take the blame. Antonio just glared over at her and called her a "whore" for getting in the car.

"Just like your mother!" his words spewed out.

Patricia looked down in shame, knowing she had done nothing wrong but allowed his words to affect her. She felt like a prisoner in her own home. After that, the bus was to be the only means of transport for her. She recalled the incident in third grade, sentenced to stay indoors for making a friend in school. *Oh no, not this time.*

From then on, she ventured to be more clever. When an opportunity to go on a health class field trip arose, she knew her parents would never agree to it. So, she simply forged their signature on the permission slip. Her health teacher was an attractive young lady, full of laughter, always joking. The field trip was to the downtown underground tunnels. She wondered what the underground tunnels had to do with health. *No matter, it would be fun!* She thought. The class gathered in a café, and Ms. Jones, the teacher, handed them a small bottle of what looked like red juice. She told them it was okay to drink; a special gift from her. Patricia drank hers and, before realizing it, felt woozy, happy, and warm inside. Laughter poured out of her. She was talkative and engaging in conversation with her classmates. The others drank theirs too. It was the best field trip ever!

They all made it back to the classroom, the day ended, and she took the bus home just as instructed. By the time she arrived home, the woozy feeling was beginning to wear off, and she worried that her parents would know that she had lied, and worse, she had gotten drunk. But luckily, no one was home. She rushed inside and took a shower. As she was getting dressed, Maria arrived, asking her about her day. Patricia simply said, "It was the same as always."

CHAPTER 7

Careful What You Wish For

Patricia laid in bed with Maria. The sun had just set. Tony was at football practice and Elizabeth was tucked away in bed. They were talking when they heard the front door suddenly open and then slam shut. Antonio was home. Maria quickly got up from the bed and went to the kitchen. Antonio was angry and intoxicated. He demanded to know where his food was and why no one had waited for him to get home to eat with him. On most nights, he was too obliterated to even notice. But this time, he did notice and demanded answers. He stood in the middle of the room with his black Dickies pants and blue uniform shirt. On the right-hand side of his uniform was a patch with his name. His clothes were always well pressed, and his hair slicked back, glistening with gel. "You're a lazy, good-for-nothing bitch" he yelled at Maria. "If it weren't for me, you wouldn't even be here. You'd be on the streets. I rescued your ass!" Maria had always stayed quiet when

Antonio went into a rage, but she didn't relent this time; she began to argue with him. Things got heated between them, and Antonio raised his hand, prepared to strike her. And then he stopped with his hand in midair. There was a different energy in the room; he no longer seemed to command it the way he usually did. Maria recognized this change in Antonio's demeanor and found her power.

"Just leave, get out of the house!" she demanded. Patricia had been standing in the hallway leading into the kitchen, watching. Slowly, she moved closer to Antonio. Overwhelmed with fear, anger, and hate, the filter between her brain and her mouth disappeared.

"I hope you die!" Yelled Patricia into his face.

Antonio got in his Porsche 944, a gift he had just purchased himself, and sped off. "Who do they think they are?" he repeated to himself. With nowhere to go, he headed towards his shop, speeding down the road, weaving in and out of lanes. Cars were honking and flashing their lights. He was blinded, unable to see the other vehicles. He raced towards them, closer and closer until he collided head-on with another vehicle. His car rolled and landed upside down near a gas station.

Dragging his body out of the car, he managed to get the attention of a stranger. Words barely escaped his mouth.

"Call my daughter, Patricia." He was able to give the stranger the phone number before he was taken away by a life flight.

The phone rang. The stranger asked to speak to Patricia and told the thirteen-year-old that her father had been in a very bad car accident.

"He is headed to Memorial Hospital via life flight." Patricia dropped the phone. Her face turned pale as she looked up at Maria and said, "I killed him."

Maria looked at her in confusion and begged her to explain what was going on, who had been on the phone. Patricia sobbed as she managed to re-tell Maria the words she had been told on the phone.

Maria packed up the family, and they rushed to the hospital. Inconsolable and blaming herself, Patricia repeatedly said, "It's my fault. I wished him dead."

"He should not have been drinking and driving and definitely should not have been going the wrong way." Maria tried to console an inconsolable Patricia.

They arrived at the hospital to see Antonio hooked up to several tubes. Machines were beeping as several nurses surrounded him. Finally, one of the nurses walked over to them and told them he was in critical condition and might not make it through the night. They rushed him to the operating room for an emergency open-heart surgery. The steering wheel had crushed his chest and damaged his heart valves.

The driver of the other vehicle, a high-profile politician, was nowhere in sight. He requested to be taken to a different hospital to avoid the media. The rumor was that he was in the car inebriated with a prostitute. *What were the chances? Two drunk drivers, one with a hooker in tow.*

While Antonio was in surgery, Patricia walked down to the hospital chapel.

"God, please save him. If he lives, I promise to be nice and do whatever he says." Just as she was speaking, a rush of cold air hit her. Unaware of where it came from, it startled her. The lights began to blink on and off, and she felt a sense of peace. She could feel whoever or whatever was watching over her. It gave her the strength she needed to calm herself and reflect on more positive thoughts. Feeling connected to the source of energy enlightened her and kept her from drowning in sorrow or fear. The guardian angel that watched over her had not failed her.

With a new sense of hope, she walked back to Antonio's room. Maria, Elizabeth, and Tony sat in silence, waiting for Antonio to return.

The doctor entered, informing them the surgery was over and went well. Everyone's face softened with relief. Still, no one said anything.

The three of them knew what they were thinking. Antonio's survival, relinquishing them of guilt, but simultaneously they wished the outcome would have been different, granting them a peaceful life.

Overcome with empathy for Antonio, Patricia would spend every minute by his bedside. He laid there so helpless with little to say. She had never seen her father vulnerable. It made him human and approachable, capable of giving and receiving love. Her thoughts raced with hope. *Maybe this will allow him to be a better father and love me for who I am.*

The day came when he could go home. Besides having what looked like an oversized zipper on his chest, Antonio was on the road to recovery. Patricia remembered her promise. She would cook for him, bring him the paper, and read to him. At first, he was very subdued, but his recovery not only came with better health but also with a return of his violent outbursts and toxic rhetoric. Heartbroken and disappointed, Patricia couldn't keep up with his violence, no matter what she had promised.

"Sorry, but I just can't do it." She told God that she was done taking care of Antonio. Once again, she felt like a failure.

As always, luck was on Antonio's side; he suffered no repercussions from the accident. It was as if it had never happened. Apart from the scar on his chest, all evidence of the accident disappeared. No ticket was ever issued. The politician in the other car, made sure that he would never be traced back to the scene of the accident, freeing Antonio from any liability or punishment.

Antonio returned to work, and he needed help at the shop.

"I need someone to answer the phone, create invoices, and talk to the customers." It wasn't so much that he was asking Patricia; he was telling her that she would be doing these things. Reluctantly, she agreed. The work atmosphere was, at best, horrible. The shop was dirty, and the men working there would all stare at her lecherously. She started to see her father in action and realized he was a completely different person outside the house. He would joke with customers, laugh, and engage in intelligent conversations.

"They love him," Patricia reported to Maria.

One day, a customer came in and started to talk to Patricia flirtatiously. Antonio caught it and became infuriated. He sent her to clean the bathrooms. *Anything but the bathrooms*, she thought. The bathrooms were worse than any garbage dump. *Playboy* magazines were stacked up high to the ceiling, and they were also full of Schlitz beer cans, Antonio's drink of choice. No way was she going to touch anything in there. She simply slipped out. The piles of papers reminded her of her grandmother's bedroom in El Salvador, and she became nostalgic. She wondered what would have happened if they had stayed in El Salvador. *Would their lives have been better off? It definitely could not have been any worse!*

The drinking started at noon. Antonio emptied one beer can after another until it was time to go home. Different people would come by to engage in conversation and share a drink with him. People from all walks of life; police officers, lawyers, and doctors somehow found their way to him. He was like a celebrity to them, but none of them knew who he really was. In other people's eyes, he was a great dad, husband, and successful business owner.

"Antonio, what a great man, you are teaching your daughter to work!" She overheard things like that numerous times. Little did they know he was a terrible father and husband, and the reason she was there was because he could not keep an office manager to save his life. They did not know of his rages, temper, or ways of humiliating his family.

Antonio had agreed to pay Patricia for her hours at the shop. However, week after week went by, and she never got a dollar. Whenever she asked him about it, he would say he would pay her the following week. Hearing him say, "I'll get you next week," became like hearing a broken record. Meanwhile, he walked around with hundred-dollar bills in his pocket, handing them out to his employees so they could buy more beer. She wasn't surprised, he had never kept his word, and she knew he never would.

One Saturday evening, just before Christmas, they were going out for dinner. A dinner night out was never pleasant. They had chosen a place called Luby's, near the mall, so they could take Elizabeth to see Santa Claus afterward. Antonio made Maria drive, so he could drink on the way there, while at dinner, and on the way back.

"You're driving too slow."

"You're too close to the other cars."

He'd continue to belittle Maria until they reached the restaurant— all the while with a beer in his hand.

Once they had sat down and their food arrived, he started in on Tony.

"You're so fat. Are you going to eat all that?"

"Leave him alone," Maria would interject.

"It's your fault he's fat. You baby him and make him a wimp. Look at him. He is a lousy good-for-nothing. He is never going to get a woman." He kept going on. Tony would not say anything; he held his fury inside because his fear of Antonio was all-consuming.

Antonio then shifted his malice to Patricia. She cringed, knowing what was coming.

"Look at those fat thighs, just like your mother." He grabbed her thigh and shook her.

"You've always been fat. And your hair, when was the last time you brushed it?" Patricia could no longer take it. She stared at the iced tea sitting on the table. Her face turned red as she felt the anger rise. Something took over. In slow motion, her hand trembling, she reached for the iced tea and threw it in his face.

"Enough!" she shouted. Drenched, drops of iced tea fell from Antonio's hair. He sat in silence, his face reflecting total shock. Maria,

Tony, and Elizabeth just stared. Everyone was waiting for him to blow up, but he didn't. He did not open his mouth for the rest of the night. Everyone in the restaurant stared at them as they got up from the table and walked out. No one said a word on the drive home. When they arrived, he went straight to his room, shut the door, and stayed there for the rest of the night. After that, there was no discussion of the incident ever again.

Patricia was waiting for her mother to say something to her, but she didn't. Something had cracked inside her today. Antonio's constant badgering was exhausting for her and the entire family. He was a bully, and she was tired of being his punching bag. She needed to stand up to him, or he would never stop. Whatever happened from that moment forward, she knew there was no going back to the way things had been before.

CHAPTER 8

Rabbit Stew

The Houston heat and humidity were fierce, and the summer months were the most brutal. It was the summer before freshman year, and Patricia started to become more conscious of her appearance. People were constantly commenting on her weight. Being rail-thin was in fashion, and she was curvaceous. Unfortunately, her Middle Eastern roots did not match Western standards of beauty. During her doctor's visits, the doctor would always say, "Make sure you eat from the four food groups. You need to watch your weight." Along with Antonio's constant negative remarks about her body, that did not help her self-esteem. To make things worse, she was going through puberty, and Maria never explained what her body was going through. She had no idea what to expect or how her body would change.

She wanted to wear cute shorts and strappy tops but could not bear to show off her body. Wearing bathing suits or any clothes that showed her skin was out of the question. She would instantly become embarrassed. If she were going to the beach, she would wear long shorts and have anxiety when taking her clothes off to get in the water. Her curves, thick legs, and tiny waist stuck out.

"Stop eating!" Antonio would say to her. So, she stopped eating. Going up to ten days without food was not unusual for her. When she did eat, she would punish herself by starving herself afterward. Finally, she started to lose weight and then began to work out. In front of the television, she and Maria would exercise to Jane Fonda's videos. She would also go running in the neighborhood. She was losing weight, but she found no satisfaction with her body.

Still, Patricia wanted to lose more weight. She would look in the mirror, and all she saw was the overweight child that her father yelled at constantly. But to everyone else, Patricia was getting too thin. The customers at the shop asked if she was sick. The more comments she heard, the worse she felt. Eventually, the starving stopped, but her image in the mirror was still of an overweight girl. She weighed barely eighty pounds, but that was not enough. Patricia could not control her environment, but she could control what she put or didn't put in her mouth. Becoming thin gave her the power to disappear. For the first time, she was doing exactly what she wanted. No one could tell her she had to if she didn't want to eat. So the next time she went to the doctor for a checkup, he told her to eat.

"You're too thin," the doctor proclaimed. Patricia just stared at him with a blank look. At that moment, she did not see herself as a person, but rather as a weapon to control and destroy anybody and everybody telling her how she should be.

"I am just fine," replied Patricia. "I'm eating when I want and do not need anyone to tell me different." The doctor looked at her with concern but more so with shock as she had never said more than yes or no. "Don't bother talking to my parents. They don't care what I do. It's my body, and I'll do as I please."

The already cold room became colder. There was total silence, but Patricia felt powerful. She had stood up for herself and was not going to listen. Finally, she had found a method to deal with the madness.

The doctor simply smiled and documented the visit. "I'll see you next time. Remember the four food groups," he said as he walked out of the room.

Patricia got dressed. She felt something she had never felt before—a sense of control.

Getting off the examination table, she glared over and saw her reflection in the mirror, her ribs protruding through, you could count each one, her stomach sank in, almost touching her back. It was a sight that would worry most, but it was her suit of armor, one she would wear with pride.

Patricia was eight years older than Elizabeth. Elizabeth was a beautiful, feisty girl with light brown curly locks, light skin, and brown eyes. She was brilliant. She was also overweight. Elizabeth had many friends and a positive attitude. Being heavy did not stop her, nor did it affect her.

Since she was the youngest, Elizabeth had escaped most of the raging madness from Antonio, and Maria had softened quite considerably as Elizabeth grew up. Maria had more time to dedicate to Elizabeth than her two older children. Antonio, for all intents and purposes, basically ignored Elizabeth. She didn't get his brutal rage, nor did she really get any attention from him. In that sense, he treated all his children equally—he didn't show much care for any of them.

Elizabeth would pick on Patricia, silly things like pulling her hair or pinching her skin. Anytime Patricia would speak up, Maria would say, "You're the oldest. Don't fight with your little sister." As the baby, Elizabeth always got privileges that neither Tony nor Patricia got. She was rarely in trouble and had no chores. Maria and Elizabeth were glued at the hip. They were only apart when Maria was at work and Elizabeth was at school. Maria gave in to anything that Elizabeth wanted. While Patricia was cooking or washing dishes, Elizabeth would sit in her room, playing or watching television. One set of rules applied for the older kids and another for the younger child. There was also one set of rules for boys and one for girls. Being a middle child and a girl was just not in Patricia's favor.

Despite the competition and fighting between the two sisters, Patricia always watched out to ensure Elizabeth was safe and secure. She took it upon herself to make sure that no harm, no matter how hurtful Elizabeth could be, would come to her baby sister.

Elizabeth was friends with Cindy, the neighbor's daughter. She was closer to Patricia's age but enjoyed spending time with Elizabeth. Cindy's parents worked all the time, and she would often be home alone after school with her two brothers. The family had many cats living in their home, and it had become a problem. Cats were also sleeping in their car and often died in the house without anyone knowing until an intolerable stench emanated from the place. Eventually, they'd find the dead feline bodies and bury them in the backyard.

The family didn't let anyone go over except for Tony and Elizabeth, out of embarrassment. Patricia didn't particularly want to go to their house; the overabundance of cats grossed her out. But she liked the family, they were friendly and seemed to love each other, and their sons were nice. Well, as nice as teenage boys could be. The families had lived next to each other for years but hardly interacted outside of the occasional wave from the front yard. The neighbors feared Antonio, having seen and heard too many of his rages.

Tony was in the Future Farmers of America club at school. As part of their activities, he had to raise small animals—feeding, studying, and observing them. So Tony decided that taking care of rabbits would be his project. He had to bring the rabbits home with him and take care of them there. Patricia wasn't thrilled. She didn't have much of a penchant for rabbits. Rabbits, rats, and cats; she didn't like small critters.

One evening, Patricia fell asleep on the couch, as she was prone to do. Still suffering from nightmares, she frequently dozed off watching television, exhausted. It was early, and the sun had not yet set. Her nightmares always followed the same pattern and never seemed to stop: the door opening, the weight, and then transitioning into another place and time. Only this time, she felt something jumping on her. Sitting up, startled, she realized it was the rabbits.

"Get them off of me!" she screamed. "Help! Help!" She leapt up and jumped on top of the couch, kicking the rabbits away.

"My rabbits!" Tony came running into the room, "Leave my rabbits alone!" He picked them up and took them back to their cage in the garage. As the children gathered in the living room, Elizabeth admitted she had been playing with the rabbits earlier in the afternoon and had forgotten to lock their cage door when she put them back. She also left the door between the garage and the house open.

Thankfully, they were home alone, and their whooping and hollering had gone unnoticed. When the chaos ended, the three kids sat down in a fit of laughter. They looked at each other with amusement as Tony said, "Don't let Pops see them. He'll make rabbit stew." With that, they laughed even harder.

CHAPTER 9

Fresh Beginnings

Freshman year began, and Patricia was still working for Antonio at the auto repair shop. She had heard about a new grocery store opening, and she wanted a job there. She needed to earn some actual money. Maria drove her to the store so Patricia could fill out a job application. Her mother knew that Patricia needed an outlet, and a job was a good thing. She wanted to be a cashier, and all cashiers had to pass the employment exam along with a math test.

The testing location was in a room above the store. Patricia climbed the narrow stairs and found a woman seated behind a wooden desk; she was distributing the job applications and math tests. The old lady wore glasses that sat on the bridge of her pointy nose, and they framed her wrinkled face. When she looked up, her eyebrows almost touched her forehead, and her lips were painted red.

"May I help you?"

Patricia froze. She was intimidated and nervous. Her heart was pounding so hard that she could hear the beats inside her. She tried to speak, but no words were coming from her mouth.

"Speak up," the woman said. "Are you here for an application?"

"Yes." Finally, the words tumbled from her lips.

Patricia took the test sheet from the woman's hand and found a place to sit. She couldn't focus, and the numbers became a blur to her. Her mind was racing faster than her heartbeat, unable to concentrate or contain the anxiety that set in. She got up and ran out of the room, down the stairs. Then she tripped and fell on the last step, tumbling onto the store floor. Tears were streaming down her face. *I'm a total failure*, she thought. *I'm going to have to go back to that dirty shop. That's my destiny.*

As she ran out the sliding doors, she bumped into a man and fell again.

"Are you okay?" He picked her up and looked at her with kind eyes.

"No," she replied. "I just applied for a job here, and I could not pass a simple math test."

"Well, we will see about that," replied the stranger. "Come with me," he said. "Let me introduce myself, my name is John Harding, and I am the owner of this store."

Mr. Harding walked with her back up the stairs, passed by the old woman at the table, and sat Patricia down at a desk. He then placed a pencil and a clean test sheet in front of her.

"Take your time," he said calmly. "Come see me when you get your grade." He was an older man with gray hair and a loving disposition. His demeanor had a soothing effect on her. As he passed by the woman at the desk, he uttered under his breath, "Behave yourself."

Patricia finished the exam and handed the test to the woman. She waited anxiously as the woman's eyes scrolled down the page.

"You passed."

Patricia ran down the stairs, found Mr. Harding, and handed him her test.

"You start next week," he said with a smile.

Patricia was so excited, and she didn't know how to contain it. But then she remembered she'd have to tell Antonio, which brought her back to earth.

"He is not going to let me work anywhere else," she woefully said to Maria that night.

Patricia felt like a prisoner; she spent all night dwelling on her situation. On the one hand, her father did not offer emotional stability. Monetarily, he supported the family, but forced her to work for no pay. She was aware the family business needed help, but Antonio's actions were not to work as a team or a family. On the other hand, it had to do with control; constantly having something to hold over Patricia's head.

She went to bed, imagining herself working at the store, making new friends, and feeling happy. Patricia held onto the image until she started to fall asleep. She began to ask for help to free her from the jail where she was trapped until finally, she fell asleep.

Patricia woke riddled with guilt, but hoped she would get out of the situation.

"It is Tuesday, and Mr. Harding said I would start in a week. When will you tell Pop's?" Patricia paced back and forth in the kitchen.

Maria kept chopping onions in preparation for dinner. Then, under her breath, without looking up, she calmly said, "We won't tell him for now," Maria knew it was going to be tough and did not look forward to telling Antonio.

Maria had a system. Whenever she needed to get Antonio's consent or tell him something unpleasant, she had to set it up, making it seem as if it was his idea.

Thankfully that night, when Antonio came home, he was in good spirits. Maria knew it was then or never.

Maria casually asked. "Have you seen the new grocery store coming in on the corner of 2234 and Highway 6?"

"Yes, I saw it," replied Antonio.

"They are hiring," continued Maria.

"Are you looking for a job?" questioned Antonio as he looked up at her with eyebrows raised.

"No, but I was thinking that Patricia needs to earn some money and help around the house," Maria said, looking over at Antonio with anticipation. She tried hard to hold back her fear.

"She has a job at the shop," he again replied with a questionable look.

"Patricia is not getting paid, and nor should she." Maria caught herself, making sure to make Antonio feel he was in control. "In addition, she will get school credit for working and still have time to help out in the shop. It will also keep her from hanging out with people, especially boys."

Antonio did not answer. He ate his dinner and went to bed with no other words or mention of the situation.

The following day, Antonio told Maria that Patricia could work at the grocery store, but only 10 hours a week, and she had to keep helping at the shop. He added a warning to his consent. "If I find out she is staying out late or getting into any trouble at work, you will both pay the price. So, watch it!"

That answer would have to do. With that, Patricia would start work. She knew it would not be easy to keep both jobs and go to school, but she would learn to manage. It was better than nothing.

Patricia was nervous, always worried that her dad would rescind his permission.

She was keeping her side of the bargain by working at the shop and the grocery store, but as time went on, she was going to help her dad less and less. Eventually, she hoped to stop going altogether, but it kept Antonio at bay for now.

Patricia was working and earning money, thin and in shape. And boys were starting to take notice. With the money she made, she was able to buy cute clothes and learned how to accessorize.

Despite her changes, her biggest struggle was creating her own identity. She was always Tony's little sister, his shadow. She didn't know who she was if she wasn't that. While Tony was popular, most people didn't even know Patricia's name. She needed to find something of her own. Then she found out the drill team was hosting tryouts. *It could be my opportunity*, she thought. That's right, two left feet and all, she was going to put herself out there and try out.

"How are you going to be on the drill team?" Maria couldn't contain her amusement when she found out Patricia's plan.

"I don't know, but I'll try my best."

Well, her mother was right. Patricia did not make the drill team, but was offered a spot on the pep squad. *No matter*, she thought. *I'll work my way up*. She was excited to be part of something. Being on the pep squad meant Patricia got to wear a uniform and go to all the football games. Finally, she felt like she was beginning to fit in and feel normal.

Patricia made two new friends on the squad, Doreen and Bonnie. Doreen was short, with freckles, and was one of six other girls in her family. Bonnie had red, curly hair and lived with her mom. Bonnie's parents were divorced. Patricia did not know anyone that was divorced. *How cool is that?* thought Patricia. Bonnie was older and drove.

One Friday, between school and a football game, Bonnie invited Doreen and Patricia to her house. Bonnie and Doreen were in the kitchen for an excruciatingly long time while Patricia waited in the living room. When they finally came to join her, they offered her some tea.

"Tea?" asked Patricia. *It seems very adult*, she thought. They watched as she took a sip and then started laughing. They had made magic mushroom tea. Patricia went to the bathroom to wash her mouth out. Even though she didn't really drink any of it, she felt strange. Even worse, Patricia was mad at her friends. She had trusted them. She had dealt with enough alcohol in her family; she knew what it could do to a person. Patricia had no interest in it. Bonnie and Doreen kept drinking, oblivious to Patricia even being there, and then they finally went to the football game.

The Pep Squad sat in the bleachers during the football game and performed routines to cheer the team and accompany the cheerleaders. That night, Patricia could not keep up with the routine. The squad went right, and Patricia went left. The squad stood, and Patricia sat. The squad jumped, and Patricia fell. It was a disaster.

Spring came, and it was time for prom. She had no expectations of going, but to her surprise, she was asked to go by a senior. Joe was thin, tall, had dark hair and porcelain-like skin. He was the school drum major. The two did not know each other very well other than having a few conversations during football games. Nevertheless, he casually asked Patricia to prom in the hallway, and without thinking, she said yes.

Now she had to convince her parents to let her go. She didn't dare approach Antonio with details. Patricia merely mentioned going to a school dance with Tony. Maria didn't quite understand the concept of prom but thought it would be okay—it was a school function, and Tony would be there too. All Antonio heard was that she was going somewhere with Tony, which was just fine.

Prom was to take place in three weeks. The school was buzzing about the dance. Everyone heard Patricia was going with Joe and began to include her in the party planning; she was finally on the inside.

Joe was very kind. He'd walk her to her classes and carry her books. Unlike most boys, she knew Joe was very gentle and well-groomed.

Patricia began to hang out at Joe's house and made friends with his sisters and mother. Joe loved shopping and helped her pick out her dress and shoes. Patricia had never experienced this amount of attention. Her father was so opposite that it was refreshing.

Patricia was unsure if they were just friends or were dating. On occasion, she tried to hold Joe's hand, but he was not comfortable. In some ways, it was a relief. She liked having him as a friend and knew that eventually, the relationship would evolve. But she was just going to enjoy the attention for now.

Prom was her first school dance, or dance besides her uncle's wedding when she was five years old. Patricia confessed to Joe that she did not know how to dance. Being the drum major and all, he offered to teach her.

"Let's start with my favorite, Madonna," Joe admitted she was his idol. Joe had choreographed dances to all her songs. Patricia watched in awe as he spun around the room and showed her all his moves. *No way*, thought Patricia. *I will for sure make myself a fool.*

None of it seemed to bother Joe. He was patient and told her, "Don't worry, Follow me and you'll be fine."

Patricia started hearing about her classmates' plans to spend the night out, and some people were even getting a hotel room. It made Patricia nervous. *What if Joe is expecting me to do something. I haven't even really kissed a boy.*

As the day neared, Patricia finally got the nerve to ask Joe about their activities after prom. Joe looked at her, puzzled, and quickly replied that he had no plans other than coming home. That eased Patricia, knowing he had no expectations. But, at the same time, she wondered if something was wrong with her. After all, he had not even tried to hold her hand.

Prom finally arrived, and only Tony from their family was aware that Patricia would be going with Joe. She swore him to secrecy, but

Tony was busy with plans of his own and did not pay much attention to what Patricia was doing at that moment. He just wanted her to go away, so he agreed not to say anything and cover for her.

Tony gave her a ride to Joe's house, where she changed, and his parents took pictures. Strangely enough, no one asked about her parents. She was content having the moment to herself.

For the first time, Patricia felt pretty. Her strapless red dress accentuated her tiny waist and flared out with ruffles. Joe gave her a wrist corsage with flowers that matched the dress's color. With the help of Joe's sisters, she managed to style her hair. Her curls fell just below her neckline. "These are going to be great pictures," said Joe's mother, grinning.

Joe's friends were all people from the band, which Patricia did not know well. Nevertheless, she managed to hold a conversation and get some laughs. Prior to prom, Joe had arranged for them to eat dinner at a nice restaurant that featured opera singers. It was one of the fanciest restaurants Patricia had experienced. The night could not have been better.

Patricia, scared to go on the dance floor, couldn't get out of her head. *I am going to embarrass myself and Joe.* Before she knew it, Joe grabbed her hand and took her out on the dance floor. Then, he proceeded to talk her through it. Left, right, left, right, but all she could come up with was left, left, left. Laughing, he just kept trying, never letting her feel embarrassed—a complete gentleman.

The night ended, and Joe never attempted to kiss her or hold her hand. Patricia was still curious as to why, but relieved.

She did not see much of Joe after that night. His attention ended abruptly, distancing himself from her, leaving her confused and unable to process her feelings. Not knowing any better, Patricia blamed herself. *Was it because she had a hard time keeping a relationship? Was it because it was so painful to carry on a conversation? Why is something so easy for others so hard for her?*

Joe would walk past her in the hallway and not even look at her. Eventually, she had no choice but to accept the outcome; instead, she focused on the good. She had become known in school and was no longer a wallflower.

Much later, she discovered that Joe was not into girls; he liked boys and had asked her to prom as a decoy. Patricia was not angry; quite the contrary, she was grateful for the way things panned out. It allowed her to enjoy herself with no pressure, unlike other girls Patricia knew. Her only regret was that she had beat herself up over it.

Patricia had been caught up in her own world, and time had passed quickly. Working, pep squad, and school had taken over. She realized one day she hadn't seen Becky in quite a while. She didn't see her very frequently at the bus stop or school, and they had not hung out in a long time. Becky's transition to high school had been even more difficult than Patricia's. She spent a great amount of time dwelling on the negative aspects of her life and feeling sorry for herself. Her home environment was harsh. Becky's mother had passed away when she was seven years old, and she was being raised by an abusive father. Patricia would always say to Becky, "We don't have time for sorry. We need to keep moving. If we don't move, we will be stuck here forever," hoping that Becky would be motivated to get out of her funk.

Patricia decided to walk over to Becky's house; she wanted to see her friend. When she knocked on the door, she could hear rumblings on the other side. The door slowly opened, and she was greeted by a foul stench, an overpowering odor that nearly knocked her out. Becky's father stood before her. His eyes were red and watery, his face swollen. He had never looked particularly put together, but this was a sight Patricia had never seen. It looked and smelled as if he had not bathed or changed his clothes in weeks.

"Is Becky home?" asked Patricia.

"Becky is gone," he answered.

"Where did she go?"

"She is dead."

"Dead? What do you mean dead?"

"She took her life." With that, Becky's father slammed the door in Patricia's face.

Patricia could not believe it. Becky. Her friend, Becky, had committed suicide. No one talked about it at school. *The feeling of being invisible was real*, she thought. She felt terrible that she did not check on her friend. She felt awful for moving on and leaving her behind. Becky was her first true friend, and Patricia would never forget her. If only Becky had talked to someone. She could have realized that it was possible to get past the pain, that change was achievable, that there was hope. She just had to believe. But Becky never gave herself that chance.

CHAPTER 10

All Roads Lead Out

Antonio opened an auto body shop down the street from his auto repair. To everyone's relief, it kept him busy, distracting him from the happenings at home. Maria took an interest in the business and started working as the adjuster. She was good at it. It turns out numbers were her thing. This new arrangement did not stop Maria and Antonio from fighting. He was always accusing her of taking up with other men—all false accusations. One week it was the body man; the next week, it was a customer. He would often show up at the shop yelling and causing a scene.

"You're a whore," he'd yell out to the room. Then he would get in his car and drive away. He was a jealous and competitive man. The business belonged to both of them, and he could not stand that she was leading its progress. He felt that she was interested in something other than him, and he did not like it at all. He wanted to keep her small and quiet.

Maria enjoyed her work, but it was not easy. In addition to Antonio, she faced many challenges within the industry itself. The auto business was a man's world and even though she was driving the deals, men discriminated against her. Maria would negotiate contracts with dealerships, and during the negotiations, dealers would ask to speak with the owner.

"I am the owner."

"No, your husband." They didn't even know if she was married or not, just assumed that there had to be a man involved somehow. Patricia admired her mother for continuing regardless of the obstacles she faced. It was good to see her stand up for herself. Maria was in control and had a voice after all the years of abuse from Antonio she had endured. She was proving herself among men, defying their expectations of her. Maria was more resilient and so much stronger than she had been before.

When Patricia was not at school, she'd come around the shop to help Maria or just hang out. She enjoyed seeing Maria in action and learned from watching everything she did. Her cousin, Mario, also worked there. He was the son of Antonio's older sister. Though Patricia's aunt and family also lived in Houston, they didn't particularly socialize with them. Antonio had given Mario a job, though. Mario was quiet, but he liked talking to Patricia and even offered to show her how to drive. He was older than her by five years and owned a yellow Toyota with a manual transmission. He even challenged her to learn on a stick.

"It's much cooler," Mario said. Every afternoon after school, they would practice.

Patricia would break abruptly and grind the gears, but Mario was patient. One afternoon, during one of their driving lessons, Mario put his hands on her lap. She looked at him, confused. He told her to drive down an empty street and pull over. Patricia obliged. When the car halted to a stop, he leaned over and grabbed her. She was terrified and managed to stumble out of the car. Patricia started running, but Mario caught up to her and grabbed her arm. In the process, she managed to push him down to the ground. She kept running and didn't look back. *Why does this keep happening to me?* she thought. She ran back to the shop crying, then sat alone in silence. She kept going over all the things she had said and done. *He is my cousin, for goodness sake.*

She avoided Mario at all costs, but he continued to work at the shop, and she couldn't help but see him. Every chance he got, he would try to corner Patricia and touch her. She was disgusted and fearful. She never told anyone, remaining silent. *No one will believe me.* She bore the burden of his actions. Another person she trusted had betrayed her.

Patricia's 16th birthday rolled around and Antonio's estranged younger brother, Ronnie, surprised her with a car. He had lived with them for a short time and enjoyed spending time with her. Shortly after a bad car accident, he disappeared, and they rarely saw him after that. When he had heard that she had gotten her license, he used the money he received from the accident to give her the gift of a car.

Not being a very experienced driver, she weaved and bounced from lane to lane. She drove like Antonio, except she wasn't drunk. She hoped that an angel guide she may have had was watching out for her and the other people on the road when she got behind the wheel. She drove from home to school to work and back home, rarely deviating from her typical route.

Work was a priority, and having a car made it more accessible. Working at the grocery store gave her pleasure, and talking to the customers came naturally to her. The insecurities of her youth seemed to be non-existent once she put her uniform on; Patricia transformed into her alter ego. She began as a cashier and then graduated to working at the Customer Service Center. It paid better and came with more responsibilities. She worked weekends and a few nights during the week as well.

She was busy, but she also felt free and independent, and the possibility of living on her own became more of a reality. Just as Maria had taught her, Patricia saved most of each paycheck.

School was still complicated for Patricia as she continued to struggle to focus. Her mind was always wandering. She could see the teacher's lips moving, but it was as if no sound was coming out. She'd get lost and fall behind. Meanwhile, Tony was a straight-A student and popular. Life did not seem fair.

When she would feel bad about herself, old habits would kick in: she would stop eating. Finally, during P.E. one day, one of the coaches took her aside with a concerned look on her face.

"Please weigh yourself."

"Why?"

"Your weight has dropped significantly since the start of the year. We are worried you may have an eating disorder," the coach said with concern.

"I do not," she replied defensively. But, like everything in her life, she lied to hide it.

"I'll need to call your mom."

When Patricia got home from school, Maria did not mention anything, so she assumed the coach never called. She was scared that she may be in trouble and ashamed of herself. She knew she could control this; she didn't see anything wrong with her lifestyle.

CHAPTER 11

Loveless Summer

Patricia loved to visit her Uncle Juan in El Salvador. He had saved her that fateful Christmas many years before and had always given her unconditional love. She visited him and his family for a few weeks every summer. The summer before sophomore year, Maria decided to send Patricia to stay with her uncle to learn Spanish. Even though it was her first language, Patricia had started forgetting it, and Maria wanted her to learn about their culture. Patricia was excited to fly by herself and spend the summer with Juan and his family. He had two kids; the oldest was Elizabeth's age, and the other one was a few years younger.

Uncle Juan's family life was different from Patricia's life in Houston. Juan had built and designed his own house. It was like a sanctuary, situated in a beautiful neighborhood outside the city with lush, green gardens surrounded by mountains. He was a gentle, caring man who treated his family with respect, shared in all the family duties, and was heavily involved in his children's lives. Juan was a talented artist with a full-time job in an advertising company. His wife, Emily, was complicated, dominating, demanding, and often sarcastic. She was critical of Patricia, always commenting on how she should dress, conduct herself, talk, walk, and even eat. Emily considered herself "high society" and had no problem making everyone around her very aware of that. Her parents owned an all-girls school where Patricia attended classes while she was in town.

Patricia was excited to see Emily this time since Patricia was thin and had a whole new wardrobe to show off. The entire family welcomed Patricia at the airport, and Emily, as expected, was ecstatic to see the changes in her niece.

"What an improvement," were the first words out of her mouth.

On the way home, they stopped to eat traditional Salvadorian food. As they arrived at the restaurant, Patricia was surprised that Emily's family had come to greet her. She hadn't expected it, and it made her anxious and nervous. Emily's younger brother, Carlos, was only four years older than Patricia and was part of the welcoming committee. Patricia had always had a crush on him. He had never noticed the chubby little girl that came to visit from time to time. But that day, when she walked into the restaurant, he took notice. Carlos immediately walked over to Patricia and started a conversation. He even asked her to sit next to him at dinner. It was surreal.

Emily's parents were there as well. They talked to her about the classes she would be taking and what she could expect. Emily also had a younger sister, Roxana, whom Patricia befriended. *It is going to be a great summer*, she thought.

Monday came, and Patricia got dressed in the school uniform. Unlike the first day of school back home, she was not nervous about going to school and meeting new people. Instead, she felt excited. Juan dropped her off on his way to work. When she walked in, everyone stared at her—she was the new kid in school, after all. The material was hard. The math was more advanced, and the writing, well, it was in Spanish. But, somehow, she was okay with it.

During lunch, all the girls rushed over to her. They wanted to know where she lived, what she did, and about America. They took an interest in her. *Is this what it's like to be popular?* she thought. Patty, a girl in her final year, walked over to Patricia and introduced herself.

"I've heard a lot about you. I am Carlos's girlfriend," she said. Patricia's heart sank. She felt a warm sensation come over her face and her hands clammy. Patricia tried to stay calm and not act suspicious, even though she had no reason to feel guilty. *Girlfriend, why does he have a girlfriend? Again, life is not fair*, she thought.

"Nice to meet you," said Patricia.

"A couple of us are getting together at my house after school. Would you like to come?" Patty was very welcoming, and Patricia couldn't help but accept the invitation.

Not wanting to like her initially, Patricia finally made a new best friend. Patricia and Patty were inseparable, attending events together, watching movies, and talking all the time. It was as if they had known each other all their lives. Patty came from a wealthy family and had everything she wanted. Her parents spared no expense on their daughter or her new friend, making their adventures that much more elaborate. Patricia grew up learning to be frugal and careful with money; this new dynamic of bottomless funds was exhilarating, but it wasn't just the endless spending. Being with Patty meant having access to a private driver, chefs, and housekeepers.

Despite the friendship she cherished with Patty, Patricia was still head over heels for Carlos. It was easy not to think about him when he wasn't around, but when the three of them were together, Patricia longed to be the one he turned to and flirted with each day. And she would have to swallow the heaviness in her chest when Patty described the intimate details of her and Carlos's romance. She knew she had to bury any feelings for Carlos and distance herself from him.

But Carlos did not make it easy. He found ways to spend time alone with Patricia. Carlos would take her on motorcycle rides and get her ice cream. He was flirtatious and gave mixed signals. After school, Patricia would go home with Emily's parents and wait for Juan or Emily to pick her up. It was during those afternoons she would sit and talk to Carlos, and their friendship grew. It was innocent, but feelings were brewing.

Torn between her new friendship and her first real love, she knew she needed to do the right thing. Her heart and conscience were in a battle between longing and logic. But the more she tried to distance herself from him, the more Carlos would pull her in.

One rainy afternoon, while watching television together, Carlos slowly extended his hand to hold hers as he leaned in to kiss her. He looked deeply at her with his sparkling brown eyes, square jaw, and dark, black hair. She got lost in the moment. She had never kissed a boy and desperately wanted to kiss him, but her conscience kicked in, and she pulled away.

He jumped up from the coach.

"Want to take a ride on my bike?"

"Okay," she nervously responded. They jumped on the bike and sped up and down the hills, taking sharp turns as they made their way to the lookout. Patricia held him tight as the wind blew on her face and her arms wrapped tighter around his waist. A euphoric feeling took over. It was all coming together; an adventure on the bike, the boy she liked, and a beautiful setting.

As they reached the top, he pulled over. The view was magical. The sun was setting, and the city lights framed the mountainside. At that moment, he turned back and kissed her. Her heart melted, and a burst of energy rushed through her body, leaving her with feelings she had never felt before.

"I know what you're thinking," he said. "But I don't love her as I love you." *Could this really be happening?* Patricia thought. Without saying a word, she just smiled at him. It was getting late, so they headed back home.

So many emotions were surging through her, and she was unable to sleep. Patricia did not know what to make of it. She was exhilarated by the kiss and was full of happiness; at the same time, she felt like a traitor to her best friend. How would she face Patty the next day?

At school, she tried to avoid seeing Patty or even making eye contact with her. *She is going to know*, she repeated in her mind. Patricia distanced herself from Patty more and more. When Patty would ask her to come over, she'd say she couldn't. Patricia spent more time at Carlos's house with the excuse that Juan and Emily were at work. Carlos also was spending less time with Patty and more time with Patricia. His parents took notice and inquired as to the state of their relationship. He said it was just a friendship.

One weekend, Carlos and Roxana invited Patricia to join them at the state fair in town. She was dying to go and asked Uncle Juan if he could spend the night at Emily's family home so that the three of them could leave for the fair early the next day.

"I don't see why not."

That night they all played games together and even had a dance contest. Carlos and his sister were masters of disco. Patricia envisioned herself in their family. It was so different from the family life she had. But unfortunately, she let her imagination get the best of her, let her guard down, and failed to see what was coming.

Patricia went to sleep that night in the room next to Carlos. They had gone to bed early to get up early the following day so they could go to the fair. She was sound asleep and woke up to find Carlos in bed next to her. His body was pressed against hers, and he was kissing her while his hands undressed her. He was moving fast, taking her clothes off. Patricia was not comfortable. Her body froze, unable to speak; she shook her head no. His body felt so heavy, so intense, and she tried to push him off of her but couldn't.

Finally, she yelled, "NO!"

He put his hand over her mouth and told her to be quiet. She cried silently and stared up at the ceiling. It was caving in. His body was sweaty, and he overwhelmingly smelled of cologne. Her head started spinning, and she became dizzy. She felt pain as he pushed himself inside of her.

Patricia was confused as to what was happening. She looked down and saw blood everywhere. It did not stop him. All she felt was pain. He emptied himself, rolled off of her, stood up, and took her by the hand to the bathroom, where he told her to clean herself. She was crying, in shock, and overwhelmed. And she had no clue what had just happened to her, but she knew none of it had felt right.

Sobbing in the shower, she tried to make sense of it all. She liked Carlos but never intended for this to happen. The image of her trying to push him off replayed in her head. She remembered motioning for him to stop and yelling no.

She stepped out of the shower and walked back into the bedroom. The room looked like a crime scene, and the victim had to hide the evidence. There was no sign of Carlos. Patricia began to slowly pick up the remnants of the nightmare that had just occurred. Unsure what to do with all the blood-stained towels, she gathered them and put them in a corner. Unable to cope, she crawled back into the bed and cried herself to sleep.

The next morning, everyone gathered for breakfast. Conversation flowed like normal. No one took real notice of the fact that Patricia was more silent than usual. It was surreal. She had lived through a nightmare just hours before, and now they were eating as if everything was fine in the world. Carlos refused to make eye contact with her. The flirtatious looks were gone. Once again, she was invisible.

Patty came to meet them at the fair, and she and Carlos sauntered off on their own. Heartbroken and unable to say anything to anyone, Patricia was embarrassed and ashamed. Roxana noticed that something was off but didn't ask Patricia if anything was wrong. She managed to get through the day but counted the seconds until she could get away from all of them.

Luckily when they got to the house, Juan was waiting to take her back to his home.

"Are you okay?" he asked. "You seem extremely quiet."

"I am okay."

She did not eat or sleep. The only thing she wished for was that the earth would swallow her alive. Patricia had two more weeks left in El Salvador; she had never thought that she would want time to speed up so she could get back to Houston sooner rather than later. She even feigned illness so that Uncle Juan would let her stay home from school.

Patricia spent lots of time sitting outside in the garden, deep in her thoughts. She had convinced herself that Carlos would call, that he would come to her. What had happened must have been normal. *It was supposed to be this way.* Her imagination had just gotten the best of her. She was probably making it out to be worse than what it was. Patricia knew she was destined to be with Carlos. He just needed time to explain everything to Patty. After all, they had been together for a long time. *It's all understandable.*

Two weeks went by and Patricia finally saw Carlos, but only at a family gathering. He even engaged in small talk with her, but they never were in a private moment for her to ask him about that night. He always made sure that they were around other people. Patricia was still convinced that Carlos was waiting for the right moment to declare his undying love for her. That never happened.

The day had come for her to go home finally. Uncle Juan drove her to the airport, and she cried all the way.

"It's going to be fine," said Juan, trying to console her. "Life at home will get better, I'm sure." He had no clue that her tears were not about returning to Houston. Instead, her tears were for everything she had lost: her love, her pride, her friends, and her virginity.

Juan parked and walked her to the counter to check in. Patricia continually looked back, but no one was there. "Is everything okay?" asked Juan. At that moment, Patricia broke down in tears. He hugged her, trying to console her. Juan was still confused about the nature of the sadness. "Do you want me to call your mom and ask her if you can stay?" Juan asked, grasping at solutions. "No!" Patricia explained as she stopped the tears and pulled herself together.

The airport was full of families to see loved ones off. Patricia watched as loneliness and anger welled up inside of her. Knowing she had to go back to Houston and deal with her family, all while keeping another secret, she wondered how much more she could bear.

Becky flashed into her thoughts at that very moment. Another friend she let down just like she let her friend Patty down.

Finally checked in, Patricia said her final goodbyes to Uncle Juan and headed to the gate. Walking through the airport tunnel felt like she was in a kaleidoscope. Colors flashed before her, but they were all meshed. Her heart raced, and her breath was shallow. She began to sweat and felt the walls caving in. Before Patricia knew it, she passed out, waking to a stranger standing over her asking if she was okay. He helped her up. Patricia assured the stranger she was fine and ran to her gate and boarded.

Even as she settled into the plane, she imagined Carlos running to catch the last seat, sit next to her and accompany her on the flight back to Houston to start a life together. Patricia felt confused and conflicted. She felt violated by a man she loved. *How could I have feelings for someone that has taken so much from me?* Yet, in the back of her mind, she still imagined Carlos coming to the airport, seeing her off, and telling her of his big plans of reuniting in Houston. But there was no such going away reception. All she had was her wounded soul and misplaced love.

DRIFTING

Born to a drifter, I drifted ashore

Full of light but unable to soar

Pumped full of insecurities and never wills

Following the heroes up the hills

One by one, letting go

Reaching the top, unable to stop

I drop to the ground, led by cries

Unable to loosen ties of the past

Realizing it makes me holdfast

It's who I am at last

Ready for more, I open the door to see the beauty;
I behold

Never again, doubtful words will I be told

Self-love is here for me

CHAPTER 12

Down the Hill We Go

Patricia returned home a different person than when she left. So much had changed. At the beginning of the summer, she felt enthusiastic about the future. She was making friends, had a great job, and was learning to drive. Within weeks, everything changed. She felt defeated. She had lost hope in the blink of an eye.

She started locking herself up in her room for hours, sleeping all day, and watching television at night. Finally, Maria took notice. "What's going on with you?" she asked.

"Nothing!" yelled Patricia. *Teenage drama*, thought Maria.

"When are you going back to work?"

"I don't know." Patricia was in no mood to talk. She'd sit in front of the television with a gallon of ice cream and finish it all. If it wasn't ice cream, it was a 28-ounce jar of Jiffy peanut butter, the crunchy kind.

She would eat the entire jar in one sitting, one large spoonful at a time. But nothing satisfied her. Patricia felt empty and needed something to fill her since she was unfulfilled with life. When her stomach was so full, and her skin stretched to the maximum, she would go to the bathroom and throw up. Her eating disorder was back. She was now controlling what was going in her body as well as what was coming out of it.

Now, every day felt as if it was the first day of middle school. Waking up, she would feel insecure about herself and unsure of what the day would bring. She would panic and feel disoriented. She would get out of bed, but the day was an endless drag.

Patricia decided she would call Carlos and make sure she was not making things up. She continuously thought about the motorcycle ride and the kiss. Then her mind would flash back to the bloody incident.

The problem was she had to call long-distance and knew her mom would not allow it. Not able to contain herself, she dialed the number anyway. Roxane, Carlos's sister, answered. Patricia asked to speak to Carlos.

Roxane recognized Patricia's voice. "Is that you?" she asked.

"Yes," Patricia said with excitement.

"Don't call here again!" Silence took over as Roxane hung up.

Patricia just felt worse. *What could he have said to everyone?* Her mind spun out of control. Her body and mind were overloaded. Once again, she started to feel as she had at the airport. Before she knew it, Patricia passed out. She recalled what happened in El Salvador, but it was as if it had happened to someone else. Like a horror movie playing out, Patricia viewed it in her mind in disgust. Only this time, she felt distanced from the incident. It gave her the strength to move forward.

While she was away, life had carried on in the Lopez household. Maria was busier than ever with the business. Patricia needed a distraction at least until school started again. She began to help her mom, running errands and helping to secure auto parts that were hard to find.

And Patricia was actually enjoying herself. The more complex the task at hand, the more satisfaction she would feel when it was complete.

As summer ended, she would have to prepare for the start of school and seeing old friends. Patricia felt differently about life and what was important to her. She no longer felt like a child. She fretted about going back to school, feeling like a huge black cloud was hanging over her head.

Finally, Patricia started her job at the grocery store once more, hoping that seeing friends there would help ease the transition of the return to classes.

As things progressed with the family business, the dynamics between Maria and Antonio got worse. They were arguing more than ever. Maria was standing up for herself with greater frequency, and Antonio could not stand it. Antonio felt it was him against the world, with no one to support him.

During the first week of school that fall, Patricia gave one of the boys from the neighborhood a ride to school. Antonio had seen this on his way to work and was infuriated. He came home drunk that night, as usual, and pushed the door open to find Patricia in the kitchen, finishing up some chores. Tony and Elizabeth were in their rooms, and Maria was folding clothes.

Antonio rushed over to Patricia, yelling, "You're a whore! I saw you in the car with that boy!" He slammed her up against the wall. She hung there, all 85 pounds, limp, and waited for his fist to meet her face. Tony only had heard the screams and came bounding from his room.

Tony had seen that look on his sister's face too many times as Antonio pounded on his mother. This time he was going to do something about it. "Leave her alone! You're not going to hurt her. Put her down!" Tony could not contain his anger, the fear in his sister's eyes growing more intense.

"Oh yeah?" replied Antonio, "Now you're man enough to stand up to me?" Antonio was not going to let anyone disrespect him, but Tony did not stand down. He played football and had lifted weights all summer. Tony, now leaner and much stronger than before, knew it was time to show his father he was not a wimp.

"I'm not backing off."

"We will see about that!" yelled Antonio. Now focusing on his battle with Tony, he dropped Patricia from his grip and went outside. Tony and Patricia looked at each other in confusion.

What was Antonio going to do? He came back into the house a few minutes later with a gun in his hand and pointing it at Tony. His eyes darted back and forth between Tony and Patricia. Antonio's insecurities that he was alone and unappreciated fueled his rage. His two children were against him.

Maria arrived in the kitchen to see the three standing there; Antonio with a gun in his hand, and Tony on the other end. Maria's fears manifested right in front of her. She was afraid a day would come when Antonio would snap, and she would not be able to protect the family.

"Antonio, put the gun down!" Maria screamed at him as her body trembled. Antonio turned the gun from Tony to Maria. For a flash, Maria felt relief. *Lord, please take me.* She closed her eyes.

"Let's take this outside!" Tony growled at Antonio. He wanted to get Antonio out of the house and away from his mother and sisters. He always felt he had to protect the women in his life, and the day had come that he was being put to the test.

As soon as Tony and Antonio were in the driveway, Patricia fled the house and ran to their neighbor's. As Patricia ran, she remembered the day in the trailer when their bodies bounced from one side to the other, and they had nowhere to run, no one to help them. Her fears mounted that they would not survive this time.

"Help, help, my dad has a gun!" She banged on the door but to no avail. She went to the next house and found that they, also, would not open the door. Everyone in the neighborhood was terrified of Antonio, and no one wanted to get involved in their domestic dispute.

"Call the police!" Patricia yelled out to anyone who would listen. She ran back to the house to find Tony and Antonio facing each other. Maria was in tears, pleading for Antonio to put the gun down. But Antonio was not going to surrender.

"You are a man. Fight me fist to fist." Tony knew the only way to get Antonio to put the weapon down was to question his manhood. Antonio put the gun down. They circled one another slowly. Antonio was preparing to strike when Tony blocked him and struck him down with a right cross. Antonio was bleeding. Tony had broken his father's nose.

Tony felt a sense of pride. He had finally done what he wanted to do years ago. Looking over at his mother and sister, he proclaimed, "I don't regret what I have done. He deserved it and more." Then he turned to Antonio, "Today, I am a man." Antonio looked up at Tony with embarrassment and shame.

They could hear sirens in the background. The police were on their way. Someone must have called them. Antonio picked up his things, quickly got in the car, and drove off.

He drove himself to the nearest hospital, where he was treated for his broken nose and received stitches for a cut on his forehead.

The phone rang at the house and Maria answered it. It was Antonio, calling from the hospital. "I'm sorry. That was my fault." Antonio's voice was low, he sounded defeated, and she could tell he was humiliated. Words like that had barely ever been uttered by him before. But the apologetic demeanor did not last long. As his wounds were treated, Antonio's narrative changed to one where he was the victim and where his entire family was ungrateful and against him.

The police arrived just as Antonio had fled. They questioned Maria and the children. All of them played down the events that had transpired. If Antonio got into any trouble, they could not imagine what the repercussions for them would be. So Maria did not file any charges, and the police did not fill out an official report. After the police left, Maria tried to calm everyone down. Patricia blamed herself, and Elizabeth was trying to understand what had happened. Tony retreated to his room. That night was a turning point in his life. A new sense of power had fueled him in standing up to his father. With that fuel, he would find new friends and develop a sense of who he was that was very different from the chubby little boy he had once been.

Antonio did not come home for a couple of weeks. When he finally showed up back at work, Antonio told everyone he had fallen on his face, a "misstep," as he called it. His face was extremely swollen, and he looked as if Mike Tyson had gotten the better of him in a few rounds in the ring. Patricia was upset, felt hopeless, and was doubtful of how they would all move on. Antonio had never been a true father in any emotional capacity and could never give her the love she craved, but he was the only father she had. His physical presence away from the house created a void. It wasn't that she necessarily missed him; she missed the idea of him. She was torn between missing the concept of a father and not wanting her real one in the house.

Patricia knew that Antonio would try to come back into the house and that Maria was never strong enough to say no.

"Please, don't let him come back!" pleaded Patricia. "I can't live with him here anymore." But just as Patricia suspected, Antonio tried to convince Maria to let him back in, so Patricia decided she needed to give her mother an ultimatum.

"It's him or me," Patricia told her mother. "If he comes back, I'm moving out." Maria was full of insecurities and doubts. She had never learned to live independently, and she would need to learn. However, she knew that Patricia was right; Antonio had become a cancer and was ruining their lives.

Similar to Tony, Maria was tired of the bullying. She knew it was time to stand up to Antonio. "You're not coming back. We are moving forward without you." It took all of her courage to say those words to Antonio. While Antonio stared at her in anger, he knew he had no choice. Too much had happened.

"You will all fail without me." He stormed away from the house. Maria didn't know what the future would be like for them, but she knew that she could not let what had happened ever happen again.

CHAPTER 13

Newcomers

Patricia sank deeper into depression. She had lost complete interest in her looks and was barely going to school. But when she did show up, everyone took notice of her appearance. "What happened?" They would ask her. *Mind your business*, she thought. She was no longer in school activities and slept through most of her classes because she was up all night. Patricia no longer cared about being popular or making friends. Her grades dropped, and her attendance was unacceptable. No one took notice of that, not a teacher, not her mother.

School felt suffocating for Patricia. Finally, she learned that a career prep course could get her out of a full day of class, but she needed to find an office job to take advantage of this opportunity. Anything would be better than sitting in a classroom with a bunch of kids who had no idea about real life.

Patricia had become resentful towards her peers. Everyone's lives seemed so much better than hers, and Patricia just could not relate to anyone around her. But when a job as a receptionist at a doctor's office appeared in the school newspaper, Patricia quickly asked to fill out an application and set up an interview.

During her interview process, the office manager, Rose, asked her why she wanted to work in such a serious job rather than stay at school with her friends. Her reply was, "I have no friends. My entire life has been about survival. I feel more comfortable dealing with people with illnesses and despair than with entitled teenagers who have no sense of reality."

Rose respected her answer and hired her on the spot. The setup was perfect. She could leave school at noon, go to the doctor's office for a few hours, and still keep her job at the grocery store on nights and weekends.

The busier Patricia kept herself, the less she had to think about her misfortunes. Unlike school, she could relate to the patients who came in with various illnesses. She started to get relief from talking to the people she was checking in and out during the day. Their faces filled with sorrow and hopelessness. Patricia had good health, but everything else was rotten. At the moment, she did not realize that good health trumped an awful life. With good health, the rest could fall in place. With lousy health, everything would fall apart.

The doctor's office was an excellent experience for her. While she failed at school, she excelled at work. The words that did not make sense to her in school made sense at her job. She felt useful, with a purpose. Patricia's favorite patients were the elderly. They were so happy to have someone to talk to, and Patricia was delighted she could make them happy. They fueled her.

With that fuel, she gained confidence. She was a quick learner, and they soon offered her a promotion filing insurance claims, but she could not stay at this job forever and knew she needed to finish her education.

Back at school, she never stopped feeling like an outcast. There was no motivation, and the classes all seemed senseless to her. Having never found a true niche of friends, she started to hang out with a crew of kids who loved to party. They shared one thing in common—a dislike for the institution they found themselves sentenced in.

Patricia's new friends would host keg parties out in open fields on weekends. With Antonio no longer at the house, she had no one keeping an eye on her comings and goings, and she felt free to do whatever she wanted. Maria implemented a midnight curfew for her, but it was hardly ever followed. She began drinking, not caring about the consequences. Patricia found that drinking would numb her, and all her insecurities and fears would be pushed down, at least for the moment.

One night, at a house party—whose house it was, no one seemed to know—she noticed someone she had never seen before. *He must not be from around here*, she thought. So she asked around, and her suspicions confirmed that he was from the neighboring subdivision.

"His name is Rob," one of the girls she was hanging with said. He wasn't particularly good-looking, and she found out he was a known troublemaker. Maybe that was why she found him so intriguing. He was dangerous. He had wavy, black hair and dark, soulless eyes and was wearing work boots. They locked eyes, and Rob made his way over to Patricia. It wasn't long after that they began dating. Rob had quit school and worked to help support his family. He smoked pot and drank heavily. Rob became Patricia's on-again, off-again boyfriend for the next three years. As far as bad decisions go, this was a pretty big one.

Patricia spent most of her free time at Rob's house. He and his three siblings were raised by their single mother. Their father had left the house years prior, and their mother worked two jobs just to stay afloat. Patricia and Rob's mother did not get along. His mother thought that Patricia was a distraction but later learned to tolerate her presence.

Maria had no level of tolerance for Rob. She despised him. He came to pick up Patricia at the house one time; Maria only had to look at him once to know she wanted nothing to do with him. Her radar told her that Rob was not a good man. Her relationship with Antonio put her on alert; she did not have a good feeling. The more Maria told Patricia of her dislike of Rob and how she did not want her to spend time with him, the more she pushed Patricia toward Rob. Maria and Patricia had their issues and disagreements in the past, but nothing of this magnitude. Mother and daughter were being driven farther and farther apart. Patricia continued to save the money she was earning; she wanted to leave the house as soon as possible. Even with Antonio out of the picture, her home life was miserable. Too many things had happened to all of them. Patricia was still a child, and Maria still acted like a child.

While Patricia and Maria were at each other's throats, Antonio found a new home near his shop and found a new mate, too. Jen was a nursing student. She was originally from Philadelphia and had moved to Houston to attend nursing school. They met when Jen had car problems, had brought her car to the shop, and proceeded to tell Antonio a sob story about not having enough money to pay for the repairs. She was attractive, tall, slender, had long brown hair, was 10 years younger than Antonio, and needy. *Perfect*, he thought. Antonio acted like a gentleman around her and charmed her with his wit. Before long, Jen was working in the shop. Maria was convinced that the younger woman was after Antonio's money.

Tony wanted nothing to do with Antonio; he had not seen his father since the fight. Antonio never reached out to Tony, and Tony refused to go to the shop and interact with him. On the other hand, Patricia was guilted by Maria to have a relationship with Antonio. For all the abuse Maria had endured because of Antonio, it was a mystery why she forced her daughters to spend time around the man.

"He is still your father, and you have to respect him." She couldn't understand her mother's reasoning. Antonio was a monster. Patricia would reluctantly go with Elizabeth to see him on a regular basis. Because of this, Patricia slowly started to form a relationship with Jen. Jen was young and fun, and showed her some attention. It was all she craved. Jen listened to her, and Patricia felt comfortable talking to her.

Jen convinced Patricia that Antonio had changed, becoming a better person.

"He just needed understanding," she'd always tell Patricia. Jen believed it was her mission to rescue Patricia. She'd invite Patricia to the home she shared with Antonio to spend the night, and Patricia gladly went as it was a great way for her to get away from Maria. The destructive behavior Maria and Antonio had once had in the Lopez house was replaced by similar behavior between Maria and Patricia.

Jen's "parenting" skills were less than conventional. Jen and Antonio would take Patricia to the local bars and drink with her as if they were all friends. They would even sneak her into clubs. Patricia, barely 16 at the time, thought this was the best thing ever. Jen was desperate to be Patricia's friend. She had no clue about the consequences of exposing someone so young to an adult world. One night, they had all gone out and gotten extremely drunk. Patricia drove home hammered.

Maria was awake and waiting for Patricia upon arrival. Patricia was visibly drunk, and Maria yelled at her about the obvious dangers of drinking and driving. When she asked her who she had been out drinking with, Patricia could not lie—she told her that it had been Antonio and Jen. Maria was beside herself; she could not contain her anger. It took all her willpower not to get in the car at that moment and drive to Antonio's house in the middle of the night.

She waited until the morning, put Patricia in the car, and drove to the shop. Patricia waited while Maria bee-lined it to Jen and started yelling at her from across the room.

"You have no right to take my daughter drinking and let her drive home."

"She is old enough to take care of herself." Jen seemed to have no care in the world about the events of the night before. They were arguing back and forth, and Patricia watched as Maria encroached upon Jen, and Jen's body was slowly moving backward. Antonio was watching too, but he was too great a coward to get involved in a catfight.

Jen was tired of arguing and finally blurted out, "Enough! Get a life. Let Antonio and his children be happy." The words hit Maria like a dagger. *Who is this outsider telling me how to run my life?* Her head was on fire, and she wasn't thinking straight. She picked up a glass ashtray on the counter and launched it at Jen. Jen ducked, and the glass shattered against the door behind her. You could hear a pin drop as everyone stopped what they were doing. Some customers left, not knowing what would happen next. Patricia was still in the car, watching from the window.

Maria was furious and went after Antonio next.

"You and your little girlfriend better stay away from my daughter!" she yelled. "You have done enough damage, and I won't let you do anymore."

Patricia was never of care or concern to Antonio. All of them were mere pawns in his game. He had a new girlfriend in Jen, Patricia was a playmate for her, and he had also managed to get under Maria's skin. Antonio saw nothing wrong with the situation.

"Leave! You are out of control! You almost killed Jen!" Antonio finally spoke up and was yelling at Maria.

Maria was not satisfied. She was angry and wanted vengeance. Maria looked over and saw a money bag ready for deposit sitting on the counter. So she grabbed it and ran towards the car. The only thing Antonio cared about was his money. She knew taking the bag would get a reaction from him. Maria was right. Antonio was quickly on her heels and running after her as she fled towards the car. She threw the bag of money at Patricia through the open passenger side window.

Antonio grabbed Maria by the arm and pulled her back.

"Give me back the bag," he screamed into her face. Flashes of the violence she had seen between the two of them before swarmed in Patricia's head. Antonio had a tight hold on Maria and was twisting her arm, pulling it behind her. Maria's face was red and pinched tight with pain. Patricia opened the bag that was in her lap. There was a gun inside. Antonio always had a gun in the bag of money when he was going to make a deposit. Patricia knew this.

Now in a panic and knowing she needed to help her mother, Patricia grabbed the gun and pointed it at Antonio, tears rolling down her face, her arm trembling. Antonio looked up and saw the gun pointing at him. He released Maria, and she scrambled into the car and drove off. There was silence for a long time as they drove. It was Maria who was the first to speak.

"I won't put up with any more disrespect from you. If you want to live with Antonio and his girlfriend, go!" Patricia remained silent. Some things were better left unsaid.

The scene between Maria and Jen, and then between Maria and Antonio, had left Patricia a complete wreck. She had pointed a gun at her father. *How was she any different from Antonio when he pointed a gun at her family?* And at that moment, Maria could only think of her own needs. Patricia's entire life had been complete chaos with no adult to steer her. She was searching for compassion, guidance, and, most of all, acceptance and love from her parents. But the adults in her life had no awareness or direction for themselves; there was no way they could give those things to her when they did not possess them themselves.

CHAPTER 14

Truth Be Told

Life was spinning out of control. Patricia was a living, breathing human but a complete shell of the girl she once was. She was skipping more classes and falling further behind in school. With no friends at school, she gravitated towards a boy who skipped classes as much as she did. Johan was short and chubby with slicked-back brown hair.

Johan knew that Patricia had a car and was gullible. He convinced her to give him rides, telling her that his mother needed him to help her with deliveries. He claimed they were very important deliveries and would always make Patricia wait in the car while he would take packages from place to place.

On one ride, Patricia got tired of staying in the car and went into the house. She walked up the stairs, followed the voices she heard, and opened the door to a bedroom. Johan stood there with another boy from school. She recognized him but didn't know who the other kid was. On the table was a bag of cocaine.

"What is this?" she asked, knowing but needing confirmation.

"It's just a side job we have," Johan replied as he dismissed her. "Wait in the car." Unaware of his relationship with the other boy or the business they were running, she knew she needed to distance herself. She decided then and there to no longer give him any more rides, and he soon stopped speaking to her.

Apart from school and work, Patricia did everything possible to stay away from the house. Maria would tell anyone who would listen that Patricia was a lost soul.

"There is no helping her," she would say to everyone, even when Patricia was in the same room. It was as if Patricia did not even exist, and her privacy was no longer a concern of Maria's.

Patricia felt like an outsider in her own home. Her relationship with Tony had dwindled. They barely spoke, and she was just another problem for him. Elizabeth was also distant. Even at her young age, Elizabeth absorbed what Maria would say like a sponge, was critical of Patricia, and kept her distance.

Patricia would stay out late, usually with Rob, and drink. Though he and his friends were into drugs, she never went near the stuff. It scared her. For Rob's birthday that year, his brother held a get-together at his apartment complex and rented out the pool area, along with several kegs of beer.

Everyone was drinking and having a good time. Patricia was standing dangerously close to the edge, talking to Rob's brother. Someone thought it would be funny to push her into the pool. Instead of a clean fall, Patricia hit her head on the edge of the pool and began to sink further to the bottom. Like all those years before, she saw the rays of light, heard the laughter of children playing, and saw the glistening lake. She could hear the garbled sounds of the people above, "Get her out!"

Someone jumped in and dragged her out. She laid on her back and, again, like years before, thought to herself, *Would it have been better to stay at the bottom of the pool?*

When Patricia finally stood up, she dried off and, with much embarrassment, walked to her car. Before leaving, she sat in the car pondering over the events. Everything was a struggle in her life; nothing was simple, and nothing was positive. *It's supposed to be the best time of my life*, she thought, *But instead, I am inundated with obstacles. What is the universe trying to tell me? Was there a particular reason I had to pay this price?* She was too young to realize that she was raising herself; there was no one supervising her or setting boundaries. She had no one to teach her good versus bad decisions. What made things even worse was that Rob never came to check on her to make sure she was okay. *Was I not worthy of love?* Finally, she called it quits for the night and went home.

The following evening, Tony brought a friend over. Patricia recognized him from the afternoon she had seen him, Johan, and the cocaine. He recognized her, too.

"Hey, I've seen you with Johan," he burst out.

"No, not me," she denied it. Later that night, she could hear Tony and Maria whispering. She knew she was in trouble. They called her into the kitchen, and Maria confronted her about Johan. Tony knew Johan and that he was no good. He had no clue that Patricia would have been involved in any of Johan's dealings.

"I was at the wrong place at the wrong time." Patricia felt the walls closing in on her, and she couldn't catch a break. Maria started in on her.

"You are nothing but trouble!" Maria yelled at her. "I'm so disappointed."

Patricia could no longer hold it together. Everything was falling apart. She was falling apart. She fell to her knees, and the sobs began. Her chest was tightening, and she was gasping for air. She couldn't hold it all in anymore.

"I just want to die! Somebody raped me, and I'm worthless." Tony and Maria stared at her. They were shocked into silence as Patricia was wailing. Maria knelt by her side and picked her up off the floor. She needed answers and began to question her daughter. Patricia began to unravel the previous summer's events and told her mother of her feelings of guilt, shame, and responsibility.

Maria was speechless. She continued to listen as Patricia told her everything about Carlos and how she had been violated. Then she put Patricia to bed. Maria was not a particularly empathetic person, but she saw and felt Patricia's pain. Maria had to find out the truth. She called her brother, Juan, and asked him if he had known about the events of the summer and told him what Patricia had said.

"That's not possible. The two of them were inseparable. But Carlos would never, could never, do such a thing." He agreed to talk to Carlos and get his side of the story. As expected, Carlos denied the entire thing and said that Patricia was making the whole thing up when he rejected her advances towards him.

Maria hung up. She often did not believe her daughter, but this one time, she knew Patricia was telling the truth. The pain in her voice was just too intense to make up.

Juan and Emily decided they would make a trip to Houston and talk to Patricia in person. She was making some serious accusations against Emily's brother for things that had happened while she was in their care. Patricia was apprehensive about the visit. She felt like everyone was going to gang up on her. Her whole life, she had kept everything to herself. And for good reason. No one had ever believed her. She doubted that anything would change with this revelation.

Patricia felt so ashamed that she walked around the house with her head down. She could not look Tony in his eyes. She felt his disappointment in her. On the other hand, Maria laid off Patricia for a while and did not hound her for every move she made.

A few days passed since the phone call, and Juan and Emily arrived in Houston armed with a plethora of questions, all directed at Patricia's motives and behavior.

"It could not be rape," said Emily. "You were both flirting, and you obviously liked him. My family is not like yours. The community knows us and respects us. My parents run an all-girl school, for goodness sake." Emily went on to defend her brother, "You just have a lot of mixed-up feelings because of the way you grew up. Your family has nothing to lose, but mine does. We are not dysfunctional. That is your world, not ours."

Juan said nothing. He did not defend Patricia, he just sat as his wife degraded his family and called his niece a liar. Then, without any resolution, they left the next day.

Despite their verdict, Maria still believed her daughter. She could see it in her face and knew something had happened. The visit from her uncle and aunt had left Patricia even more devastated. Her Uncle Juan was more of a father to her than Antonio had ever been. He had shown her love from the moment she was born—and had abandoned her. He would not even look at her as they left the house. She felt like a disgrace, as if she had brought shame upon her family. His betrayal of her was almost worse than what Carlos had done.

CHAPTER 15

There is No Winning

Antonio and Jen got engaged. In order for them to be married in the Catholic church, Antonio needed to have his marriage to Maria annulled. Maria refused out of sheer spite. After everything that had happened, she did not want to give him the pleasure. After waiting months for a different outcome, Antonio married Jen through other means. No one was at the wedding; no one was there to witness the affair.

To say that Antonio's relationship with his children was estranged would be an understatement. Tony refused to have anything to do with him. Patricia would try to make an effort, stopping by the shop to say hello. She wasn't even sure why she continued to do it; the outcome never changed. He would always be belligerent towards her, and his drinking had escalated to an even more dangerous level. Elizabeth would visit Antonio and Jen every other week and would stay with them on weekends.

Elizabeth usually never talked about her time with Antonio and Jen when she got back home. But one weekend, she came back and told everyone that she had seen Antonio push an eight-month pregnant Jen down the stairs. It would have shocked most anyone to hear something so brutal, but this came as no surprise for Maria and her older children. They had known that it was only a matter of time before Antonio's true colors were shown to his new wife.

Maria never remarried or even had a boyfriend. She became hyper-focused on what was going on in her home. This created even greater strife between her and Patricia. Patricia was becoming more and more destructive and would often act out. Patricia would find any excuse to not physically be in the house, preferring to spend time with anyone else.

"You don't care about us. Everyone else is better than your own family," Maria would constantly say things like this in the heat of an argument. She was both jealous and sad. She felt like she never even saw her daughter anymore. And Maria was right. Patricia would sneak out of the house, because any place was better than being around the house. She never felt love from Maria. When Patricia was surrounded by other people, she saw how functional families interacted with each other. She saw respect between adults and children; she saw love. Patricia would never share these things with Maria. She knew it would only make her mother irate.

Maria had never been shown love or empathy growing up. She was not able to give something that she had never witnessed herself. However, she believed that love came in the form of protection—such as giving her children a roof over their heads and shielding them from as much of Antonio as she possibly could. She also believed that love was shown from giving material things, since her children were never for want. Patricia desperately needed pure, unconditional love, and she looked for it everywhere. People who met Patricia genuinely liked her, but that feeling was no replacement for the love of a parent.

Patricia learned that she could get away with things. Just as she was able to lie and get away with it, she also found that she could steal and get away with it. Patricia had developed a skill for manipulation. There was a sense of innocence to her that resonated with others, and she used it to her advantage. She could get people to feel sorry for her and then have them do favors for her. Her instincts were sharp, and her wit was quick. She may not have been book smart, but she was street smart and knew how to survive. Her entire life had been about survival.

As a junior in high school, Patricia felt more like an adult than what she saw in Maria. It became harder for her to respect her mother's rules. Patricia felt trapped, and Maria was always mad at her. She was always in trouble, and she hardly ever knew why. There were no clear structures to follow, but there were high expectations that had to be met. *Was I supposed to stay at home and keep my mother company?* That was her job as a child. *Was I supposed to be a straight-A student?* She wanted to, but her mind was so cluttered and distracted that she couldn't be.

Maria had never learned to parent. She was reactionary and went too far with her actions. It was hard to tell if Maria strived to embarrass Patricia or just lacked awareness and understanding. Once, when Maria suspected that Patricia was having sex with Rob, she went to the doctor's office where Patricia worked and spoke to the nurse instead of talking to her daughter about it. When Patricia arrived at work, the nurse pulled her aside and handed her a pack of birth control pills.

"Your mom came by. She is worried for you."

Patricia was mortified and wanted the earth to swallow her whole. *Why would she not just talk to me?* She was hurt and confused. But that was just how Maria was.

Patricia was never right and could never win against her mother, so why even ask for permission for anything? She decided she would just do as she pleased, damned the consequences. For example, when her friend's sister was getting married, Patricia was invited to the wedding. Usually, she would have been gripped with fear and anxiety at the prospect of asking for permission to go to that kind of an event, let alone actually showing her face there. But for this, she figured it was time she just did it. So, she said yes to the invitation and asked a friend for a ride.

The event did prove to bring all of Patricia's social anxieties to the surface. She started drinking to calm her nerves and just continued drinking to help numb herself as the night wore on. The girl she had come with was nowhere to be seen, and Patricia assumed she was without a ride home. Her last resort was a boy she didn't know, but he seemed to be the last man standing and, without any other options, she accepted a ride from him. It was past midnight as they approached the house, and her anxiety returned, not knowing what Maria's reaction would be.

Maria was waiting in the driveway, stone-faced. Patricia took one step out of the car, and before she could thank the boy for the ride, Maria was right next to her, shoving her to the ground.

"You are worthless! What kind of decent girl comes home past midnight? Who knows what you've been doing!" She was screaming, and Patricia was sure the neighbors would hear the commotion. The boy drove off, not knowing what else to do and not wanting to get caught in Maria's wrath. Patricia lay on the ground, looking up at the stars. She felt nothing. No pain, no tears. She only felt numb. She picked herself up, walked past her mother, and walked into the house and to her room. She knew she had to leave this place. She just didn't know how to make her exit.

Soon, a Walmart opened nearby and was in need of evening stockers. She applied and got the job. Now, with three jobs bringing in money, the idea of being able to leave the house and go out on her own seemed like more of a reality. She worked through that entire summer, forgoing all social activities in order to save money.

Summer flew by, and Patricia was starting her senior year of high school. Tony had graduated at the top of his class and gotten a letterman jacket for football. He was working and attending college, all while living at home. As both he and Patricia had jobs, Maria made them pay rent to live in the house.

"Nothing in life is free," she would cooly say.

The tension between Patricia and her mom was as destructive as ever. Tony tried to keep the peace. He felt responsible for his mother, who was constantly crying to him about how she could no longer handle Patricia's out-of-hand behavior. Tony pleaded with Patricia to get her act together so they could all just create some peace. *But why is it my job to make things right?* Patricia always wondered. She had been cheated out of a childhood, and she was angry. Patricia deserved better than what she got. She could never grasp Maria's possessiveness or the anger and resentment she had towards Patricia. Maria constantly said that she had tolerated Antonio for so long, "for the kids' sake." *Was this why she was so mad at me? Was my mom's horrible life because of me?* Because, in all honesty, they would have been better off without him from the beginning.

It was time. Maria was taking Elizabeth to Disneyland and was leaving Tony and Patricia at home. While Tony was at work one day, Patricia took the opportunity to pack the car with her clothes and shoes. She had no plan beyond packing the car and getting her stuff out of the house. Patricia had some money in the bank but no place to go. First, she drove to Rob's house and asked if she could stay with him.

"No way," said his mother. "That woman is crazy." Rob's mother did not want to have anything to do with Maria. Next, she tried a girl at school, Miriam, with whom she had bonded due to their similar family backgrounds. Miriam was Hispanic and had a very religious family who was very strict with her. She was even forbidden to go out. Patricia drove to Miriam's house and asked if she could stay with her. Miriam's mother agreed, but only for a few nights. It was better than nothing.

She had to act fast. A few days at Miriam's house would fly by, and she knew Miriam's mother would not tolerate her wearing out her welcome. She had a fake ID that said she was older and could rent an apartment. Since her jobs all checked out, she was able to move into her own place. She had no furniture, nothing to sit or sleep on, not even a fork to eat meals. But that didn't matter. She finally had her freedom.

School was her next obstacle. Rumors began circulating that she was living on her own, and those rumors eventually made it to the principal's office. He called her into his office one afternoon.

"Are you living on your own?"

"Yes, sir."

"Well, you can't attend school unless you have a document stating emancipation." Patricia would have to call her mom and ask to be emancipated. She could only imagine the blow to her plans that would await her.

Patricia put the call off for days. She imagined her mother as vengeful and denying the request to prove a point. Patricia had two weeks left before the deadline. Rather than call, she decided to have the document mailed to Maria and gamble on the outcome.

Patricia continued to attend school while wondering what her mother would do.

At the same time, Maria wondered about Patricia and what she was doing. As a matter of fact, she thought Patricia had quit school. But that was not to be, as she quickly found out from the letter she received from the county asking to emancipate Patricia.

In Patricia's mind, she was an emancipated teenager. She would live on her own and continue with school; whether her mother signed off or not was irrelevant. While she wanted to graduate with the rest of her classmates, she was fine with whichever outcome.

Graduation day came and it should have been one of the happiest moments of her life. She had been through so much, endured so much torment, and had managed to finish high school on time while also working three jobs. And now, she was ready for whatever was next.

She never received notice whether Maria signed the document releasing her to her own accord, but she decided to attend graduation despite the uncertainty. As each student went up to receive their diploma, they were cheered on by friends and family.

Patricia sat in silence; she held her breath and shut her eyes. She imagined her reaction when they did not call her name. As the scene played out in her head, the announcer called her for the second time, until she finally reacted when someone nudged her to wake up. "They're calling you!"

Patricia jumped up, stepping forward to receive her diploma. There was silence in the crowd. Not one member of her family was there to witness this momentous occasion. Tears of what should have been a joy, but instead were of disappointment, streamed down her face. She assumed, no matter what they all had been through, that her family would have shown up for her that day. She had gotten what she wanted: she was alone.

Living on her own, it wouldn't be hard to imagine throwing parties and hanging out with her friends. But Patricia had no desire for that. She simply craved a life with no chaos. She had always felt misunderstood. Now, on her own, she was hoping to find some clarity.

She remembered all of those times when she would sit in her room by herself, and all she wanted was a hug. Some sign of affection telling her that, no matter what, things would be alright. If only her mother could have loved her and not treated her like yesterday's garbage. Patricia had been drowning and silently screaming out for help. But no one had been willing to listen to her.

Graduation was a momentous moment for her. She realized that Maria had let go of her hold by signing the emancipation documents, but that also meant she was officially separated from her family. She missed them, but it was time to find healthier relationships.

CHAPTER 16

All Work and No Play

Working three jobs did not leave Patricia with time for much else. She wanted to continue with her education, but there just wasn't time, and money was also an issue. She quit her job at Walmart in order to pick up a different one at Walgreens—it paid better. She was not ready for the realities of real life, but she was going to figure it out.

She walked to work in order to save gas money. Her manager at Walgreens noticed this and asked her about her life and background. She found it easier to lie than tell the truth. She was ashamed of her reality. So, she told him that her family lived in another country; she was in the US by herself and was supporting herself alone. The manager took pity on her and was compelled to help Patricia, offering to send her to pharmacy school and pay for it.

"No, thank you." Patricia was grateful but unexcited, "I don't want to be a pharmacist." She may not have known what she wanted, but she certainly knew she didn't want to be a pharmacist.

She learned that lying could lead to opportunities. She told everyone at the grocery store that her family had gone back to El Salvador after her father had been hit by a car, had gotten amnesia, and needed full-time care that they were not able to provide him with at home. The store took pity on her and let her get her groceries there for free. Her lying and stealing began to escalate. At the doctors office, sometimes, when patients paid cash, she would not report the full amount and, instead, pocket some of it herself. It helped to pay the rent. She was not proud of herself, but she had to survive.

Her personal life was nearly non-existent. She and Rob were a couple by label only—she had no time for him. He had no ambition and wasted his time on booze and drugs. His job transferred him to Dallas, and it was the perfect time to end things between them. He had never made Patricia a priority and was not headed down a healthy path. Patricia knew she deserved better. Rob was nothing but trouble. Maria had been right.

Antonio and Jen were busy raising their new baby, and Antonio remained unaware of anyone else, including his other children. Patricia continued to stop by the shop on occasion, and Antonio would give her money from time to time. She gladly took it. But nothing had changed with his attitude or actions. One afternoon, she was at the shop and noticed he was drinking more than usual, his speech was slurred, and his walk was tilted. It was a sweltering summer day, and Patricia was wearing shorts and a t-shirt. She was chatting to the new office manager, a nondescript yet pleasant man. Afterward, when she was walking back to her car, Antonio ran after her, yelling.

"You come here dressed like a whore. Talking to random men and shaking your ass." His anger was unfounded and made no sense. Not that anything he said had ever made sense. He threw a $20 bill in her face. At that moment, Patricia realized that she had voluntarily shown up there that day. She was no longer forced to see her father. She had done so of her own free will, and she didn't need to do it anymore. She had the power to walk away and never look back, which is exactly what she did. Though she would see Antonio around town from a distance, that day was the last time she spoke to her father.

As time passed, Maria began making attempts to reach out to Patricia. She missed her daughter and had been reflecting on the things that had led to their broken relationship. She realized that it was possible that her own past, pain, and lack of parenting skills had contributed to their situation. If she could help to bridge the distance between the two of them, maybe it could make up for some of the pain she had inflicted.

Initially, Patricia was reluctant to let her mother back in. She had ended her relationship with Antonio and was fully prepared to no longer have anything to do with Maria also. But, as time wore on, she gave in. Maria was trying, and Patricia was open to it. Maria offered to help Patricia go to college. Patricia was interested in being a court reporter, and there was a school specializing in that just outside of town. Maria drove her there and helped her to enroll. Within nine months, Patricia had dropped out. Like high school, this also became overwhelming for her. She couldn't concentrate when her mind would be bombarded with random thoughts; the professors spoke, but she had no clue what they were talking about; everything was confusing to her.

Patricia started going back into a depressed state of mind. The past was quickly catching up to her. She had suppressed so many emotions and simply decided to move on. Her mind was not on board; it wanted to bring up the pain.

Patricia began sleeping all day. She quit her job at the doctor's office and picked up more grocery store and pharmacy shifts. Motivating herself during the day was impossible, but these shifts were at night, and she was able to get through them without too much difficulty.

Her favorite place to sleep was on the living room couch, but she continued to have the same nightmare from childhood no matter where she slept. A door opened, and a heavy feeling came over her body. But now she could see herself in the dream—she was floating, looking down at herself as she slept. She would desperately try to get up but never could. It felt as if someone was always pulling her back down. She'd hear someone knocking at the door, and her floating self would answer, never able to see who it was. She would wake up in a cold sweat.

It was becoming harder and harder for Patricia to function night or day. She was constantly sad and feeling like she was sinking. Finally, Patricia gave into Maria's request and began to see a therapist. She never spoke in her sessions. She refused to talk. As the sessions progressed, her anxiety increased. Thoughts of the past and the reality of the present were colliding. Therapy was another thing that seemed overwhelming. So she quit.

Then Patricia quit all her jobs and focused on finding one good-paying job. She had a series of random positions that she would excel at most. She was a night auditor at a department store, a receptionist at a recruiting firm, and a file clerk at a law office. She just couldn't make any of them stick long-term.

One job had her going south of Houston to a manufacturing plant. She was a translator at the plant, translating assembly instructions from English to Spanish. It was lucrative, but, once again, the environment was toxic. Patricia was the only non-Anglo person working in the office, and the owner was a racist. He forced her to stay late after she had finished the work she was hired to do and would put a mop in her hand—Patricia had to mop the floors before she left for the day. But the money was good, so she didn't quit; the rent needed to be paid.

One morning, driving to work, she saw a burning cross in someone's yard. *Strange*, she thought. She had never seen anything like that before. She asked some of her co-workers if they knew what it was all about. No one said anything, and she felt as if she shouldn't ask about it anymore. Later, Patricia overheard that the owner was possibly involved in the cross-burning, and the town paper printed an article about how the local KKK group had been sending a message to a young white woman who was engaged to a young Black man. She was not surprised by this news; the entire town seemed to have a racist undertone to it. One night, the owner told her to mop his office floor before she left for the day. In his office, she found a white hood. She resigned immediately and never went back to that job.

Next, she tried a job at Bono's, a bar and restaurant. It was on a busy street in a bougie part of town. The day she walked in to fill out an application, the owner happened to be the one doing the interviews. Before she even had a chance to fill out an application, the owner called her over.

"What's your name?" he asked.

"Patricia," she answered.

"That's my daughter's name. You're hired."

It was the easiest job interview she'd ever had! She was hired to work behind the bar, serving drinks. Patricia had no experience serving drinks, only drinking them. And it was a busy bar; the after-work crowd would file in after their jobs finished and drink until the traffic died down and they went home. It was an oil and gas crowd who had a lot of money to spend. She could never keep up with the orders.

"Rum and Coke with a twist," someone would shout.

"Jack and Coke," said another.

She never got it right. The guy with the rum got the Jack, and the one who wanted Jack got the rum. They'd sort it out on their own and just smile at her. Despite all the confusion, the tips were great. The bartender tried to teach her some tricks, but she remained rather hopeless. She couldn't even open a bottle of wine, and the customers would have to do it themselves. The order of a cappuccino resulted in the espresso machine exploding. The customers just smiled at her, unsure whether to pity her or just reciprocate the big smile Patricia always had on her face.

Maria wanted Patricia to succeed; she needed a win to relieve her guilt. Maria knew a woman whose husband worked in management for an airline and thought that might be something Patricia would be interested in pursuing. The woman responded after Maria's inquiries regarding Patricia getting an interview there.

"You need to call Mr. Escobar at Aeromexico," Maria insisted to Patricia.

A very untraditional interview soon took place after. Mr. Escobar asked her to pick him up for lunch.

"Just drive in front of the building at noon and pick me up. I'll be wearing a gray suit," he had said to Patricia over the phone.

So Patricia showed up at noon. A slender, gray-headed man wearing a gray suit got in her car. His hair was long, and his eyebrows were wild. He instructed her to drive to the Chinese restaurant down the street. There was a lot of small talk and some questions about her experience.

"Do you speak Spanish?" asked Mr. Escobar.

"Fluently," answered Patricia. That was the extent of the questions about her skills. The lunch ended, and they drove back to the office. She dropped him off in front of the building, but instead of getting out of the car, he reached over, put his hand on her thigh, and tried kissing her. Patricia immediately moved back and removed his hand.

"Come to work Monday at 9:00 a.m.," he said. And with that, he got out of the car and walked into the building. Not sure what to make of the situation, she wondered if it was worth showing up on Monday.

But she did show up. And she kept her distance from Mr. Escobar. Soon after she began her job, he lost his on the grounds of sexual harassment allegations. Patricia was a reservations agent and would remain there longer than she expected. The schedule was flexible, and she decided it might be the right time to try her hand at school again. She took the early work shift and enrolled in evening classes. Things were taking a turn for her.

CHAPTER 17

What Else Can Happen?

Work was fine but monotonous, and Patricia was taking marketing classes at night. School continued to be a struggle for her—focusing was not a strength that she possessed. She imagined herself as a writer, and she was constantly coming up with creative stories, but the discipline to put thoughts to paper eluded her. When Patricia wasn't working or taking classes, she did little in her downtime. It was during those moments when her mind would wander to her memories of childhood; things she still was struggling with mentally. Images of the violence she had seen and endured; the yelling would echo in her head, and the chaos was always present. Scenes played out, but she was disassociated from them. Therefore, she never really dealt with the feelings they represented.

She had no one to share these things with; friends were few and mostly superficial. Her inability to trust was severely handicapping her life. But she was definitely not invisible; her co-workers took an interest in her.

Now in her early 20s, Patricia knew she needed a change, and a colleague, Linda, seemed like the perfect person to give her that opportunity. Linda was looking for a roommate as her lease was up for renewal. Patricia's place was far from ideal—it was small, the rent was high, and the commute to work was long. She and Linda worked opposite schedules and figured that living together could be a good thing; neither would be in the way of the other. They found a two-bedroom apartment across the street from the office. Neither Patricia nor Linda had a boyfriend, so they didn't have to worry about that being an issue, and they were able to have friends over on evenings and weekends.

Another colleague, Caroline, wanted to set Patricia up with a friend named Jeremy. She introduced them at a party. Jeremy was 23, tall, had piercing blue eyes, blonde hair, and a very calm disposition. He was accustomed to women fawning over him, and Patricia could tell. She had no interest in him or his attitude. Since Patricia was not initially susceptible to his charms, he became even more intrigued by her.

Patricia was not interested in a relationship. Her past experiences proved that she had difficulty feeling love, and connecting with some-one required too much work and attention. Yet Jeremy persisted. He would deliver flowers to her at work and show up to surprise her and take her out to lunch. They were all grand gestures, but Patricia never quite felt comfortable with his approach. Caroline supported Jeremy in his pursuits; she wanted Patricia and Jeremy to be together so that she and her boyfriend could double date with them.

Mardi Gras Galveston was upon them, and Caroline invited Patricia and Jeremy to join her and her boyfriend at the festival. Patricia was reluctant but finally gave in. The day was perfect. The weather was just right, everyone was in a good mood, and they all got on very well together. Jeremy drove her home afterward and asked Patricia for another date. His persistence never let up, and she eventually began to give in. They started spending more and more time together.

Jeremy still lived with his parents. They were friendly to Patricia though his mother was an intimidating woman. She was a large lady with fiery red hair and pale skin. She suffered from bouts of depression and drank a lot. His father was a slim, kindly man with gray hair. He worked overseas half the year and was not a constant presence in their home.

They lived outside of downtown in an evolving neighborhood, Second Ward. Built in the 1960s, his house was a modest shotgun home with two bedrooms, two bathrooms, a living room, and a kitchen. When you walked in the front door, you were greeted by the entire living room. There was little in the sense of privacy, but they all seemed to manage just fine.

Jeremy's family had their fair share of dysfunction. Jeremy's younger brother had drowned in Galveston when he was eight years old. Though no one spoke much about him, Patricia could tell that there was a great deal of guilt surrounding his death. Jeremy also had an older sister who had once been married to a narcotics officer, had an affair, got involved in drugs, and later remarried an engineer and had a daughter with him. Though Patricia got along fine with them, she never felt completely at ease; there seemed to be too many skeletons in their closet.

Patricia had begun to develop a keen sense of reading people and situations and found that she could predict outcomes before they happened. She believed that Jeremy was a stepping stone, someone to help her break out of her shell. Knowing that, she subconsciously would distance herself from him, never letting herself get too close because she knew the relationship would one day fade away.

Still working for the airline, Patricia decided that a trip abroad would be a good idea. Maria had always wanted to go to Spain, so they planned a week-long vacation together. Patricia felt that it could give her and her mother an opportunity to bond. Elizabeth stayed back with

Tony and was not happy that her mother and sister were going away and leaving her at home.

"I hope your plane crashes," Elizabeth shouted at them as they left the house. Not much had changed.

It was the first time in Europe for either of the women. Patricia had planned and paid for the entire trip, including hotels, trains, rental cars, and airfare. The adventure (and drama) started as soon as they took off from Houston. Maria excused herself to go to the restroom, saying she was not feeling well. Patricia had settled in, reclined her seat, and put in her headphones. Then an announcement was made.

"We need a doctor. Is there a doctor on board?" Patricia paid no mind; after all, she was not a doctor. 20 minutes went by, and Maria was still not back. Now, Patricia was concerned. She turned around to look in the direction Maria had gone in and saw someone carrying Maria back down the aisle. Maria had passed out in the plane's galley while waiting for the bathroom. The one glass of wine she had went straight to her head, and she fainted. They chalked it up to the excitement and the fact that she wasn't much of a drinker. The trip was off to a stellar start already!

They arrived in Madrid in the dead of winter, and the weather was cold and rainy. Patricia had rented a car since they would be driving through the country. They were never really ones to plan for logistics and had no clue of the driving protocols in a foreign country, so they ended up getting lost numerous times. A 30 minute trip to their hotel turned into a two hour ordeal of one wrong turn after another.

With the sun shining the following day, they decided to ditch the car and walk through the streets of the town. As they walked down the main Avenida, a car drove through a large puddle and drenched Maria. She was soaked in mud, was losing her temper, and her sense of humor was dwindling.

"What else can happen?" Maria asked out loud. As if on cue, a bird flew over and pooped in her hair. It wasn't just any poop; it was a dump so large it covered most of Maria's afro-style hairdo. Patricia could not contain herself and started to laugh hysterically. The rain had started again, and the bird excrement was now dripping down Maria's face. Maria was miserable, furious, and demanded that they go back to the hotel. So much for a day in the city!

Food and meal times proved to be a challenge. Neither were particularly thrilled with the cuisine choice in Madrid; the rich dishes they came across were not of their liking, and they mostly stuck to eating Spanish tortillas—the kind with a simple egg omelet with ham and onions. Moreover, with the Spanish siesta, most restaurants were closed when Patricia and Maria were ready to eat lunch at midday; and the locals did not even think about eating dinner until near midnight. The women just could not adjust to the time change in eating.

They left Madrid and drove south, stopping in towns like Seville and Cordoba. Maria was becoming more tired with each locale, having mood swings, bouts of anxiety, and panic attacks. Unable to sleep, she would pace back and forth in the hallways of the hotels where they stayed. During the days, she would be agitated and tired, and she began to bicker with Patricia. For her part, Patricia did her best to try and ignore Maria.

One day, while out shopping, Maria started in on Patricia. Patricia had yet to buy any souvenirs for Elizabeth or Tony back at home, which triggered Maria. She accused her daughter of being selfish. An argument ensued, and Patricia walked back to the hotel on her own, leaving Maria behind. Patricia had wanted this to be a time of bonding with her mother; it had turned out to merely be more of the same. Changing geographic locations had not changed their dynamic. It was disappointing. Patricia felt disappointed and unappreciated. She had put a lot of effort into planning the perfect mother-daughter experience, and Maria was not appreciative. At that moment, she realized that she would never be able to please her mother; nothing she did was good enough.

They drove back to Madrid the following day. The roads were winding, the sun was setting, and the views were magnificent. Patricia rolled down the windows to let in the crisp air. The smell of impending rain wafted. The mood inside the car was somber and silent. They were both exhausted and tired of each other. As they approached Madrid, the rain picked up.

Suddenly, there was a large "bang!" noise, and the next thing they knew, the front windshield was smashed. The car was spinning out of control, and Patricia struggled to keep it on the road. She eventually hit a guardrail as the vehicle came to a screeching halt. On impact, Patricia's head hit the steering wheel, but she managed to get out of the car and assess what had happened. From what she could tell, a truck carrying gravel had lost control, and the debris hit them.

"You're bleeding," yelled Maria. Patricia, in shock, had not noticed.

A bystander who saw the accident called an ambulance. Patricia got back in the car and checked Maria. Luckily, she was fine and came out unscathed. The medics tended to Patricia's wounds, and a tow truck hauled the car away.

Patricia and Maria had to take a taxi from the accident scene to their hotel in Madrid. They could not leave the country fast enough and were relieved to finally be getting on a plane home the next day. Four years later, Patricia returned to Madrid with friends, and the experience was much different. It became one of her favorite places to visit. However, Maria despised it.

CHAPTER 18

Follow the Signs

Maria returned to Houston to find more chaos. In her absence, Antonio was up to no good, scheming behind her back with the business. He had been working on a deal with a local dealership to purchase the business without her knowledge. Luckily, she found out in time and was able to act fast and negotiate a fair exit. Maria had worked hard to create something and put so much of herself into the business, but now she would be completely free of Antonio and move on with a fresh start.

Antonio's other business was not doing well, and his relationship with Jen was souring. She was the latest victim of his abuse. He was incapable of maintaining a stable relationship, and Jen could no longer take it. In a desperate but smart move, she packed up her things and moved east with the baby. Jen had family there that could support her. She left Antonio alone to deal with himself once again.

Antonio was incapable of being alone and started calling Maria to see if he could convince her that he was a changed man.

"Another chance is good for us," he would say. Maria was too aware of the damage and destruction left behind and ignored his pleas. Despite her reluctance to return to Antonio, Maria pitied him and would urge the kids to visit him. Tony and Patricia had no desire to be involved with their father, but Elizabeth still tried to maintain a relationship. After school, Maria would take Elizabeth to see her dad. Unfortunately, nothing had changed in Antonio's parenting. He had surface conversations, if one could even call them conversations, with Elizabeth and then would give her money before she left. He had never learned that money could not buy the affection of his children.

Patricia returned to the routine of work and school after the mother-daughter Spanish adventure. She was constantly nagged by something, but she wasn't sure what. She felt overwhelmingly trapped, and things were becoming too much to handle. Her reoccurring dream continued to keep her up most nights. She would wake up with a start, sweaty and feeling a heaviness on her chest.

Jeremy was her distraction. Unfortunately, he was having problems of his own. He had suffered a broken back in a car accident years earlier when the seatbelt had malfunctioned, and he continued to complain of the lingering pain from it. And work was also a struggle for him. Patricia felt sorry for him, especially with his physical condition, but she also knew he was not who she truly wanted in her life. He was kind to her and attentive, but that turned her off. She was not used to being treated this way, and it made her uncomfortable. He would always talk about the future and his plans for them after his lawsuit with the seatbelt manufacturer settled. It all seemed so farfetched to her. In Patricia's world, people worked for a living; they didn't sit back and expect miracles to happen.

Though Patricia and her roommate, Linda, hardly saw each other because of their opposite work schedules, they found each other wide awake one night. It turned out that Linda had trouble sleeping as well, confirmed when Patricia went to get some water after one of her bad dreams and found Linda sitting in the dark living room by herself. Patricia felt comfortable enough to tell Linda about her dreams, and they stayed up all night talking. Linda suggested that Patricia speak to a professional about the dreams she was having; they seemed significant.

Patricia knew Linda was right, but she still was not ready. She struggled with reconciling her past with her present. Patricia's goal was to look to the future and forget the past.

In an effort to change the way she felt, Patricia began to change her routine. She changed her school schedule and went back to work during the daytime. She also started to go out with colleagues and have a social life. There was always something happening; a wedding, shower, or just going out. No one needed an excuse to go out at that age. With all the social activities came drinking. Patricia tried to stay away from alcohol, afraid she would end up like her father, but the self-medicating helped numb her and drown out some of her feelings. Even if it did not last for long, it was gratifying.

It was the Friday before Easter, and Patricia was driving to class. She had started to doubt the meaning of life, questioning why she was alive and her mission on earth. Suddenly, she was overtaken by a sensation that she had not felt in years, one where she felt someone's presence with her, but there was no one else in the car. Patricia then became overcome with a feeling that something needed to change in her life.

Her mission was not to change socially, or superficially, it was about growing spirituality. Someone or something was there to deliver that message. The message was not spoken to her but rather delivered by an unspoken embrace, making her feel warm and peaceful.

That weekend, she went to a birthday party and drank more than she should have. To make things worse, she drove home. The next day, Patricia woke up in a panic; the night before was a blur. It was Easter Sunday, and she was supposed to meet Maria, Tony, and Elizabeth for church. It was one of the few traditions they still had. Not feeling well, but knowing she had to go, she dragged herself out of bed and got dressed. As she walked out to her car, she noticed that part of her driver's side fender was missing. Suddenly, a flash of memory came to her. Patricia had hit the side of the freeway the night before.

Patricia recalled the message that was delivered to her a couple days before in the car. How nothing happened to her and that she did not get arrested for drinking and driving was a miracle. Patricia had little regard for her own life, but the realization of what happened the night before was jarring. Living and dying were interchangeable for her, and she had become accustomed to it.

Patricia arrived at church later than the rest and could not find a parking spot. She parked away from the crowds and hurriedly walked into the chapel. Immediately upon entering the hallowed space, she was again overcome with a strong sensation. Only, this sensation was not peaceful. She began to cry without knowing why, and she could not stop. Patricia tried to control herself, but the tears took control of her instead. She spotted her family and squeezed into the pew next to them, doing her best to shield her face from them as the tears continued to stream down from her eyes silently. A cold chill had washed over her body.

As it had happened on that fateful night as a child, when she was alone on her bed and wished for help, the same presence was felt in the church. A hand touched her right shoulder, and she heard the exact words she had heard once before. *Help yourself, and I will help you.* Patricia looked around, but no one was there. She looked over at Elizabeth, sitting next to her, with her hands on her lap. Patricia closed her eyes and sat in silence until the tears dried and peace took over her.

There were too many signs for her to ignore. The energy that surrounded her was not going to let her self-destruct. She was headed down a dangerous path, and her emotions were getting the best of her. Patricia knew that she was in desperate need of the help she had been refusing for so long.

CHAPTER 19

Best and Worst Decisions

G etting help would not be easy, and Patricia pushed it aside for as long as possible. The year was coming to a close, and she was no closer to seeing a professional than she had been a year prior. She had fallen back into old habits, missing classes and sleeping late. Patricia told herself that she just had to get past the holidays, and then she would get help.

The holidays were hard for her. Patricia's childhood memories of the festive season were less than festive. Most of her feelings about this time of year were depressing. When she was younger, Maria and Antonio had taken them to the Macy's Thanksgiving Day Parade downtown. It was a chaotic scene with thousands of people. When the floats went past and goodies were thrown out to the crowds, Antonio would push Tony out onto the street to collect them. If Tony came up empty-handed, Antonio would belittle him and call him names. When someone stood too close to Maria or Patricia, Antonio would go into a rage. The day would wind down with Maria making them a meal at home and then Antonio inviting all his soccer buddies to come to the house to drink and watch football. They would all get super drunk and trash-talk their families. Christmas and New Year's were much the same, except for the most indelible Christmas, spent crossing the border to escape her father.

There was one Christmas that was memorable for its pathetic hilarity. When she was six years old, Antonio dressed up as Santa Claus. He planned to create the sounds of Santa arriving on the sleigh and delivering presents. Antonio waited until the children had gone to bed. He snuck out to get the gifts from the car. Instead of getting them back into the house without a sound, he was so drunk that he slipped on the outside stairs and went crashing down, along with the gifts, waking everyone up. Antonio quickly picked himself up and started yelling, "Ho! Ho! Ho! Merry Christmas," while simultaneously ringing a bell. He managed to get himself inside the house along with the big red bag full of Christmas presents. Tony and Patricia peeked from their room to see Santa putting the presents under the tree. As he finished, he walked out of the house once again, yelling, "Merry Christmas!" He had a flashlight in one of his pockets that he shined on and off as if Santa's sleigh was taking off. Patricia and Tony ran to the window and saw their dad taking off his Santa suit. As he proceeded to re-enter the house, they hurried back to their beds. Antonio rushed into their room with the grand announcement that Santa had come to visit. "Come on, wake up, come see all the presents." Both kids jumped up with excitement as Antonio continued with the magic of Christmas. It was a sight that Patricia never forgot.

Jeremy was getting too serious for Patricia's liking and was staying at her apartment more often. He and Linda had gotten to know each

other better and were getting along. The three of them were now spending a lot of time together. It was to the point that Patricia felt like Linda and Jeremy got along too well, but she was never one for jealousy, nor did Patricia really care for him. As Patricia was distancing herself, Linda started to make changes. She began borrowing Patricia's clothes and even cut her hair like Patricia's. The biggest change was that Linda was around the apartment far more than before. Confused about her feelings, Patricia ignored all the signs and focused on becoming stronger mentally.

By now, Patricia had found a therapist to work with regularly. Therapy was a long, slow, and arduous process. Patricia knew it would be hard; she had tried it so many times before but had never been ready. She had spent so long trying to forget so many aspects of her past that allowing herself to go back and remember them took a great deal out of her.

After weeks of work, she began to open up very slowly. Her relationship with Maria was a constant theme that came up in conversations with her therapist. Her session dug deep into Patricia's interpretation of her mother's parenting. Knowing Maria wanted to protect her children and was unable to do so was one thing, but her lack of empathy and ability to show love herself was another, along with her lack of accepting Patricia for who she was. Her relationship, or lack thereof, with Maria left Patricia feeling alone and empty. Both her parents had made many mistakes with their children, and Patricia felt she had never truly had a childhood. She knew why she was angry at Antonio, but her anger with her mother was less defined, and she did not know if it was misplaced. Unable to wrap her mind around how Maria could be a victim and a perpetrator simultaneously made Patricia feel guilty for her feelings.

When it came down to talking about Antonio and working through her memories of him, Patricia closed up like a clamshell. His violent and dismissive demeanor paralyzed her, and not being able to express those feelings created greater frustration for her. Each time she tried to work through a memory, an incident, or her recurring dream, it only created more unfulfilled silence. They would move on and talk about something else, eventually coming back to it but always having the same effect.

They spoke about Carlos. Their relationship as friends along with his betrayal and Paricia's part in betraying her friend. The therapist explained the mental confusion she was feeling.

"If you like someone and then they force themselves on you, it is confusing, but the reality is without consent, it is rape. And you have every right to feel assaulted, especially after being dismissed." It was obvious, but Patricia's lack of self-esteem made it hard for her to understand and recognize that she was a victim. As a child, she always blamed herself for the horrible actions; this was no different.

Unlike in the past, Patricia was diligent with the work she was trying to do, so she was open to all suggestions. After several attempts to break through the barriers in her mind about Antonio, the therapist suggested she go to an inpatient treatment facility.

"How will this help?" Patricia asked with much anxiety. Just the sound of it frightened her.

"It's just a clinic where you will spend two weeks in group workshops, doing exercises in addition to one-on-one therapy." Desperate for results and ready to move on, Patricia agreed. Her medical insurance at work covered the costs, making it harder to say no.

Going into the inpatient facility was one of the best and worst decisions of her adult life. She took two weeks off from work, and she called Maria to tell her.

"I'm checking into a clinic to deal with my depression and work on becoming a healthier person."

"Is it something I did?" was Maria's immediate response. "I did my best, I fought hard for you kids, and I endured years of suffering for you and your brother and sister to have everything you needed." Maria always played the victim card without giving credence to the damage done to the children or seeing their suffering.

"I'm doing this for me," Patricia replied. "And only for me."

Yet the words went to deaf ears. "I don't want anyone to know about this. Please keep it to yourself." Patricia asked kindly.

Outside of her immediate family, Linda and Jeremy were the only people who knew she was checking into a clinic. She felt embarrassed, unsure of how people would judge her. Would they think she was crazy? Would she be discredited at work or in her social circle?

Only two days after their initial conversation about inpatient therapy, Patricia was scheduled to check into the facility. The therapist did not want her to have too much time to think about it and back out. Before she left, Maria came over to her apartment and brought Elizabeth with her.

Maria cried and pleaded with her.

"Think about your decision," Maria begged her. It was as if Maria was afraid that a big, dark secret would be revealed. "Why are you dragging back the past? Do you think I am at fault? What you are doing is making me feel terrible and uncomfortable. I put everything behind me as you should. For the most part, I don't even remember the incidents. They are gone!" Maria would not stop. Elizabeth just hugged Patricia, unable to understand what was happening, but felt empathy for the situation. Maria's reaction was similar to Patricia going off to a death camp. *Death of the past*, she thought to herself.

"This is why I'm going," replied Patricia. "Because you refuse to take responsibility or acknowledge the nightmare we lived in. I've tried to forget, but my mind will not rest, and I need to be free to be a better person."

CHAPTER 20

Are Some Things Better Left in the Past?

J eremy and his mother drove Patricia to the clinic. She needed the transition to be neutral and without drama. Patricia was nervous, unsure of what to expect and how her life would change when it was over. Jeremy dropped her off at the entrance to the facility. They said their goodbyes, and Patricia reluctantly walked in. The plan was to check herself into the clinic.

Patricia walked in wearing shorts, a t-shirt, and a pair of white canvas sneakers. She carried a small bag with toiletries and a couple of days' change of clothes with her. She packed as if she was going to a resort, ready for rest and relaxation while working on herself.

Patricia approached and stopped to read the sign at the front desk. *All patients need to relinquish their personal belongings, no razors, no sharp items, no medications, no shoestrings.* This last item jumped at her. *What would you do with shoestrings?* she thought. When she was filling out the paperwork, the nurse repeated what the sign said.

"Do you have any of the indicated items?"

"A razor and shoestrings," replied Patricia.

"Hand them over," she requested.

"What for?"

"You are not allowed any items that you can hurt yourself with," replied the nurse.

"Why would I hurt myself?" Patricia asked innocently.

Patricia was processed, and a body search was done. Still extremely confused, she observed the facility as she was escorted to her room. People were walking around, talking to themselves. Others lined up for medication. She saw highly agitated people locked up in a room. She started questioning herself. *What kind of facility was this?* This is not how she pictured it. She walked by all the strange happenings and then entered a slightly calmer wing but still felt sequestered. The room assigned to her was small, stark white, with no mirrors and no bathroom, and just had two beds. Down the hall were the bathroom facilities with showers.

As the day wore on, Patricia started to get angry and anxious. She felt betrayed. She did not belong in this facility, yet she had come voluntarily. *Under the false guidance of the therapist*, her mind told her. Patricia walked out of the room and headed back to the front desk. She immediately demanded to check herself out. The staff explained that she had every right to check out but only after an evaluation by a doctor. Unknown to her, the doctor had flagged her as a risk to herself. Feeling completely out of control and stripped of her freedoms, she became even more frantic. Patricia's heart was pounding out of her chest, her breath was shallow, and she grasped at her head wondering what she had done. Pacing back and forth, she began to cry; she felt like it was the end of the road. Is this where she would have to stay forever? Once again, she remembered Becky. Then she thought about her betrayal of her friend Patty and decided she was meant to be condemned.

Once Patricia composed herself, one of the counselors walked her back. "Just settle in, come to one of the sessions," explained the counselor. "You'll feel better." *Feel better*, she thought. *I've been in prison all my life, and now I'm in another one. I'm trying to get out, not go back.* The negative thoughts wouldn't stop.

With nowhere else to go, she went to the group session. Ten women were sitting in a circle. They were all much older than her, except one that seemed young. Patricia looked around and took it all in. As she walked up to the group, one of the women was talking. The woman stood out from the others; tall, fit, and very intense. She appeared to be about 40 years old with a boyish haircut. When Patricia first walked up, the woman spoke in a deep but feminine voice, then suddenly her voice shifted to a child-like demeanor, and then a male voice.

Patricia had never seen or heard anything like this, and was intrigued by what she heard. She sat down. The woman, Billy, went into detail about the abuse she had endured from her foster parents as a child. Billy had been in the system from five years old and did not have luck with her host families. She had learned to cope with the abuse and survived by creating alter egos. Billy had developed over 50 personalities.

She was somewhat of a celebrity in the group as she had been on the "Jerry Springer Show." Everyone knew this as Billy announced it frequently. Her story was fascinating.

Patricia soon learned that each woman at the facility had a story to tell; each seemed more tragic than the one before, and they were all severe cases of abuse. Patricia took an interest in every one of their stories. Some resonated with her, while others she could not even imagine. Everyone was encouraged to talk, but no one had to share. Patricia just listened.

When the circle session was over, they all broke out for refreshments. Patricia sat back and watched, still in shock and unsure what was happening.

The young woman she had seen earlier walked over and introduced herself.

"Hi, I'm Tracy. It's your first day, isn't it? Don't worry. It gets better when you start to let go." *Let go? Let go of what?*

"I've been here a week and have one more week to go and feel much better now," continued the woman. "I've tried to commit suicide twice, so I checked myself in for the sake of my two young children." *How could this be? She looks so happy and full of life.* Tracy had long blonde curls that fell to her waist. She was slender, with green eyes that twinkled. She was not someone Patricia would have thought of as being suicidal. Patricia had lost her ability to speak. She just stared at Tracy.

"I don't know why I'm here," Patricia finally blurted out.

"That's why you are here. To find out," was Tracy's smiling response. Tracy proceeded to give Patricia the run-down on everyone. "You see that lady over there? The one with the scars on her face."

"Yes," replied Patricia in fear.

"Well, she was set on fire by her husband. Her name is Jen. Then you heard Billy talking. She has been here for four years now." *No way, thought* Patricia. With each introduction, Patricia's eyes got wider and wider.

"The Hispanic lady with the long black braids; her name is Josie. Several family members sexually abused her. Oh, let's not forget Steph; she is 60 years old. She's been in and out of this facility since she was in her 40s, suffering from deep depression. Apparently, this is the only place she feels comfortable." "Anyway," said Tracy. "You'll eventually get to know everyone."

Patricia's eyes filled with tears, feeling so out of place. She thanked Tracy for the information as she walked off.

Next on her agenda was a one-on-one session. Patricia walked in and sat down in front of the therapist. Feeling betrayed and reluctant, she decided to stay silent. Her silence did not phase the therapist; she proceeded with the session going on to explain their methods and what to expect. She went over rules and regulations and gave Patricia a prescription to take in the facility.

"You'll line up at your designated time and get your meds."

"I don't need medication," Patricia finally spoke.

"It's an antidepressant. It'll make you feel much better." All Patricia could think of was the Valium her mother had taken years before and how it had turned her into a zombie. *No way I'm taking anything*, she thought. The therapist dismissed her, and she went back to her room.

When she arrived back in the room, her roommate was back. It was one of the women in the group session, Josie, the Hispanic lady with the long black braids. Neither one of them spoke very much, and Patricia was grateful for the silence.

The schedule was strict, with everyone expected to attend several therapy sessions per day, with meals served in between and medication taken on time. When called to take the pills, Patricia simply took them into her hand and threw them away later. She was determined not to take anything mind-altering and stuck to this until the day she left the facility.

"You should take those," said Josie. "Or give them to me. I can use them later." Patricia ignored her and flushed them down the toilet.

The group sessions were becoming more and more intense. Patricia had been at the facility for three days, but it felt like an eternity. Still unable to get an evaluation from the attending doctor, she confronted him about the assessment. He responded that she needed to share her story in order to get an evaluation. Patricia was untrusting, and the whole thing felt like a setup.

During the next group session, she decided to talk, figuring she had no choice if she wanted to leave. "I don't belong here. I'm not sure why I'm here." That was the extent of her sharing.

"Welcome," said the group in unison. No one paid any mind to what she was saying. After the session, everyone walked over to socialize and talk amongst themselves. Again, Patricia felt awkward and out of place.

Jen walked over to her and introduced herself. "Hi, I'm Jen. I don't belong here either, but I keep coming back." "Voluntarily?" asked Patricia. "Yep. See this scar on my face? It's a terrible reminder of my past. I wish I could rip it off! Every time I look in the mirror, I have a breakdown that leads me to this place. Why are you here?" Jen asked.

"I got tricked," replied Patricia. "I mean, I have some things to work on, but I don't have the problems that everyone else here has." At that moment, Patricia realized what she had said. "Well, your scars may not be on the outside, but I bet you have lots of them on the inside, and they can be just as damaging and will eat you up, and eventually, they will surface to the outside on that pretty little face of yours. So watch it!" Patricia quickly excused herself and walked back to hide in her room.

On the fourth day, Patricia finally decided to be more open. She needed to redeem herself amongst the group. She was starting to feel the tension. Across from her sat Jen and Josie; they stared at her intensely. At one point, Jen looked over to Josie and whispered, "Judgy little thing, isn't she?" Josie just smiled.

The session focused on acting out a traumatic experience. There were so many for Patricia; it was hard to pick one. It was a tough crowd. She was intimidated that they would not think she was damaged enough to belong. However, Patricia started with her name. First, she told the group a synopsis of her background and then led in with her first memory of Antonio hitting Maria. Patricia acted out the memory of Antonio whipping her mother with a belt and throwing her brother across the room. As she rushed through the story, the therapist kept asking questions to draw her back in. "How did you feel? Were there any smells? Was it dark or light?" Being forced to stop and think about the answers was torturous and reliving the incident she had fought so hard to transform in her mind was painful. But despite her hesitation, as she unpacked each scene, she started to feel free from them.

Patricia was shaking and began to remember things she had forgotten. She got lost in the memory and began to transform into a child at that moment. She sat on the floor and started rocking back and forth while weeping. Jen, Josie, Billy, and Tracy surrounded her and hugged her. Patricia slowly opened her eyes and saw these women she had judged supporting her. She realized she had misjudged them.

Each time she shared, she felt better but also felt embarrassed. She thought that the group was looking through her, making her uncomfortable. She was used to hiding, as she did in the closet as a child. She had been keeping things to herself, lying to protect those around her. Finally, she realized she was protecting people who had harmed her and failed at their responsibilities. The shame was not hers to carry. It was her parents to take back and own.

After the first week at the facility, she understood why she needed to be there and gave in to working through the program. Patricia began to see herself through each woman's eyes, realizing she was not much different from them. She discovered her tendency to be self-destructive. Not working through the traumas in just two weeks, Patricia would end up coming back as many of the women in the facility had done.

Patricia decided she did not want to live her entire life holding on to baggage that would keep her down. Instead, she wanted to be happy and write her destiny.

Each character in the hospital taught her a lesson. Patricia began to bond with the women, and the women took to her; as the youngest patient, everyone wanted to help her through her journey.

Patricia needed an outlet outside of the group. At times, she would become overwhelmed with all the attention and needed alone time.

She found a park right outside the building and began to exercise. Before each session, she would go running to clear her head. It helped her mood and gave her a natural high. With each stride, she started feeling stronger and free. She was soaring. Her mind would clear, and her creativity surfaced to the forefront. Group sharing was the hardest, but she got through it with a sense of freedom after each run.

During one group session, she began to talk about her reoccurring dream. Instructed to lay down by the therapist and take a deep breath, Patricia described her feelings, what she saw, and her emotions. She closed her eyes and lost herself in the moment, and the dream began to unravel itself. The image of the person coming into her room was vivid. She understood the sensation she felt. It was all coming back to her. Patricia started to feel like she was drowning. Her mind flashed to her drowning incidents. The feeling of desperation and helplessness resembled the sensation she was having at that moment. Suddenly, her breathing stopped, her body was shaking, and she was in a cold sweat. In a panic, she thrust herself forward, and her eyes opened, and just like that, the image was gone, and she could no longer remember what she had seen. Patricia was frustrated and wanted to force the memory back.

Later, when discussing what she had experienced in her private session, the therapist advised Patricia not to force the memory, explaining that the human mind protects against bad memories and would not betray her to remember something she could not handle.

Now, even more confused, she felt it was all like a dream of a dream. During dinner, she confided in Billy. Billy urged her to let it be. "When you are ready, it will appear. 'Till then, move on."

Patricia began to feel like she needed to reach out to someone outside. She wanted to hear happy stories and catch up on what was happening at home, so Patricia rang Linda. She called the apartment, and to her surprise, Jeremy answered. "Hello, why are you in my apartment?" she asked.

"I was just hanging out with Linda," Jeremy replied. "We went to dinner, and I was heading out." She was startled but not in the mood to deal with the situation and hung up.

Her two weeks were coming to an end. She had a bittersweet feeling. Patricia was anxious but felt like she had gained helpful tools to navigate life. However, she was sad to leave the support group she had developed.

On her last day at the facility, everyone gathered around and brought a small cake. Each one wore a sign that stated, "I don't belong here." They laughed and joked about their first encounter. As each woman said goodbye to Patricia, they all gave her words of wisdom to live by and made her promise she would do her work and not return.

Patricia had a long journey ahead of her, but this was a good beginning.

CHAPTER 21

Preparing for Life

L ife after the facility took some adjusting to in the beginning. Patricia had to learn to deal with uncomfortable situations and confront them. Two items waiting for her at home were her relationship with Maria and the problem with her roommate and Jeremy.

Patricia needed to make significant changes to have a clean slate. Part of the process was to cut all ties with Maria. In order to have a healthy relationship with her mother with appropriate boundaries, Patricia needed to distance herself entirely and let Maria back in on her own terms.

The two went to lunch, and Maria listened as Patricia explained her position and asked her for space. Maria was not happy with her request. She did not respect Patricia's wishes and felt like she was being blamed, judged, and crucified for something she did not do. She was a master guilt-tripper with no boundaries. Maria had a hard time accepting Patricia's decision. Despite her daughter's request, Maria insisted on doing as she pleased, showing up unannounced at her apartment and job at all hours. She always had a pathetic look and a story to go with it. Patricia finally told Maria to stop, and that she would let Maria know when she was ready to see her; Patricia was adamant about it. Maria was upset but had no other choice.

Next on Patricia's road to a fresh start was Linda, but Linda was nowhere in sight when Patricia returned home. She had gone on a trip with her family. Patricia wanted to put the entire incident between Jeremy and Linda out of her mind, but everywhere she turned, comments confronted her.

A reservations colleague spoke on Linda's new look and how it resembled Patricia's. Apparently, in her absence, Linda only wore Patricia's clothes. Unfortunately, work was prone to gossip, so Patricia brushed it aside.

Not having seen Jeremy since being home, they decided to meet up for dinner. They met at a restaurant they frequented with a loud atmosphere and terrible service. Patricia figured it was a great place to break up with someone. She was determined to end things that night. Dinner was awkward as they engaged in small talk. Jeremy was nervous; he desperately tried to avoid talking about why he was at her apartment with Linda during her absence. However, Patricia was past that and did not want to continue with the relationship.

Just as Patricia was getting ready to tell him, Jeremy looked away and presented her with an engagement ring. "Will you marry me?" he asked. It was so out of the blue, and Patricia did not have any time to process it but knew it felt wrong. Patricia looked at him in shock. "I was not expecting this. I need time to think about it." His face dropped with obvious disappointment. "Of course," he replied. They drove home in silence, and there was no more mention of the proposal or the breakup. *Sometimes when you know, you know.* Patricia did not have the heart to tell him she did not want to see him anymore. She figured one let down at a time was more than most could handle and decided to leave it for a later date.

As Patricia tried to navigate back into her routine, she faced inconsistencies that made her stumble. Getting ready for work one morning, she realized that half her closet was empty. *Did I leave my clothes at the cleaners?* She remembered the comments from her co-workers. She walked over to Linda's closet, and there were her clothes. She had chosen not to believe the rumors, but now she had no choice but to recognize what was happening. Linda was still away, and Patricia had too many unanswered questions.

When Linda finally returned to the apartment a couple of days later, Patricia confronted her. When she asked her about the clothes, Linda looked at her as if being accused of something. "You told me I could borrow what I wanted."

"Within reason," Patricia could not believe she had to explain this.

Linda further justified her behavior and explained she borrowed the clothes to take to her grandmother, a seamstress, to make replicas. Linda did not understand why Patricia was so angry, nor did she see anything wrong with what she had done.

"Since we are on the topic of borrowing, what were you doing alone with my boyfriend in my absence?" Patricia hotly asked her. Linda's response was quick and without hesitation. "Nothing was going on. We were just having dinner together as friends." Patricia could tell she knew the question was coming, and she had rehearsed her reaction.

Linda could not look at Patricia; instead, she looked down and became very nervous. In disbelief, Patricia walked away, now sure that something was going on between the two of them.

Although Patricia wanted to end the relationship, she was hurt and betrayed. Linda had no remorse for her actions. She was oblivious and self-centered. Usually, Patricia would find a way to excuse Linda and take responsibility for her roommate's lousy behavior. *After all, I did say she could borrow what she wanted.* But this time, she tried to rationalize and remember her commitment to rid her life of all toxic relationships.

Patricia knew she needed to be strong and take the necessary steps for a healthier future. First, she asked Linda to leave by the end of the month. The second step was telling Jeremy she needed a fresh start and marriage was not in her plans. After all, they were worlds apart, and their goals and aspirations did not match.

Despite removing these people from her life, Patricia felt sad and began to feel lonely. She could feel herself going back into a depressed state of mind. When Patricia was in the facility, attending group meetings to talk about her feelings or simply listening to others would help. But, not having that option, she began to journal and put all her emotions, disappointments, and worries on paper. Patricia then started going for morning runs and trying to stay as busy as possible, but the empty feeling inside of her always hovered in the background. Patricia felt she was on a tightrope, constantly worried about falling on one side or the other with no safety net.

Her biggest challenge was making healthy relationships. The ones she had been in were toxic, and she was ridding herself of toxicity. Moving forward did not mean leaving her inner child behind. Instead, it meant helping her inner child grow to be a productive individual, one who was free of pain.

Jeremy did not let things go so quickly, he would call her at all hours, and she would simply hang up. On occasion, when she would go for a run, she would see him, until the sightings were fewer and fewer. Patricia later heard that Jeremy and Linda had started dating and were engaged. *Ironic*, she thought. *I wonder if he gave her the same ring.*

Patricia continued seeing her therapist and trying to live within the new boundaries she had imposed on herself. Finally, for the first time, she felt there were guidelines. Patricia's upbringing was wild, with no proper direction or structure and no nurturing to build confidence; not even a safe environment to do it in. The essential building blocks to create a path for healthy adulthood were never present for her and her siblings, leaving them lacking the basic necessities which now affected her. She understood it was a vicious cycle, but that was no excuse. Her parents had the power to make changes but chose not to do so. For this reason, Patricia made a conscious decision to break the cycle, learning not to repeat the same mistakes and wreak havoc on someone else's life.

Antonio had destroyed her self-esteem, instilled constant fear, took away her trust, and ripped her from the ability to be loved. She learned to hide, lie, and scheme, all to survive. Maria had made her responsible for things a child should have never been exposed to, much less assigned to handle. She was her mother's sounding board and her full-time companion, never getting any empathy or validation for her feelings of despair. Yet, despite all of this, Patricia chose to forgive. But she would never forget. Not all she had learned from Maria was bad. Maria was persistent and had a "can do" attitude about most things. If something needed fixing, she would do it herself. If there were problems that needed to be solved, they would get resolved. She was self-sufficient and made Patricia the same.

Patricia took small steps to integrate Maria back into her life, creating boundaries that they would maintain for years to come. She still had a lot to learn and work on but knowing she was on a path made her feel hopeful.

At work, she took on more shifts. Things were awkward as Linda still worked at the airline, but they managed to avoid each other. With a strong desire to succeed, she tapped into her imagination. It was a big part of her survival as a child and could serve her now as well. Applying her visualization skills to her adult life, Patricia would imagine her desire to be successful and happy, repeatedly playing out the entire scenario in her head. She dreamed about job promotions, the perfect relationship, a healthy life, basically anything she deemed desirable.

She knew not all things would happen immediately but hoped a version of her desires would manifest themselves. Patience and persistence were critical.

CHAPTER 22

Climbing Out of Her Shell

L ife was still a struggle. Patricia had many setbacks, and certain situations would trigger her. Undoing 20-plus years of abuse was not easy, but at least she had the essential tools to help her through. Still working to support herself at the airline, she made getting her degree a part-time endeavor. Relationships were still very complicated for her, and making friends was not one of her top skills.

Tired of working in reservations, she decided to seek more of a challenge. The job had become monotonous, and her yearly reviews never went well. It was always the same thing. Her evaluations noted she had no enthusiasm and was not motivated. *It is not true.* She knew she was better than that. She considered herself a great problem solver, could successfully tackle customer service issues and was a quick learner with a good memory. She efficiently tended to more customers than her co-workers. While others had to look up airport codes, Patricia had memorized them all. Her math skills also came in handy when calculating ticket prices. Her downfall was that she never let anyone notice who she really was or see her true abilities, which was mistaken for being less than capable.

She made it her mission to change her supervisor's assumptions and apply for a group department job. It was a better-paying position with more responsibility. There had been other job postings in the past, but she had never had the courage or motivation to apply. She applied for the job this time, but the manager told her she was not qualified.

She decided the response was not good enough, so she challenged management to explain why she was not eligible. They presented her with random reasons; nothing that made any sense. The work environment was nepotistic with friends and family, not qualified applicants receiving promotions. Realizing it was an obstacle that she could not change, she propositioned them.

"Give me the job, and let me prove myself. If I fail, you can fire me." *After all, what was the sense of staying in a dead-end job?* Patricia got the job and went on to prove herself.

Six months later, another opening came up as the lead of the department. Once again, Patricia put in her application, and again, this did not come without obstacles. Her supervisor was not a fan of hers, and when Patricia applied, she was told that she lacked skills. The position required advanced computer knowledge and leadership.

With much determination, she sought to prove them wrong again. Requesting an appeal of their decision, they required Patricia to pass an extensive test that had never been administered to any other candidate. Recognizing it was unfair, she was not going to let that stand in her way. It had become the norm for her, fighting for what came easily for most other people. Accepting the challenge, she stayed up all night in the office, reading manuals and testing new skills. She passed the test, and they had no choice but to give her the promotion.

During her tenure in the lead role, she implemented more efficient processes that cut the job time down to half. Now she was getting noticed, and her bosses began to give her special projects. Hope, a pretty, highly social, witty, intelligent girl, became intrigued by how Patricia had managed to surpass many of her co-workers without playing the kiss-up game.

She befriended Patricia, and the two became close. Hope was one of Patricia's first real adult friends whom she trusted and talked to, not just someone to hang out with when there was nothing else to do. It was a big step for Patricia. The two traveled to Europe, Mexico, and all the places in between. Working with the airline gave them endless travel benefits, and they took advantage of them. Patricia got to know Hope's family well. They embraced her and treated her as if she were part of the family. When Hope married, Patricia was a bridesmaid and, for the first time, felt appreciated for being herself.

By now, Patricia realized romantic relationships were too much for her to handle, so she focused on work and even took a break from school. By then, a significant management shift had taken place since she started her new position. It was a positive change with things running much more professionally. With new management came new opportunities. The airline started a new in-house packaging department, selling hotels with airfare and other services. The VP of Marketing from another airline, Lynn, came in to run the department. Since Patricia had helped streamline the group department, Lynn came to Patricia with a special project. Lynn was a native Texan who came from a wealthy family of ranchers. She was tall, about 5'8", with short, blonde hair, and always wore a power suit and heels. Lynn was newly married with small children and also a career woman who was passionate about her job.

Patricia had not encountered many women who dominated their field and worked side by side with men. Patricia looked up to Lynn.

Lynn liked Patricia's drive and saw something in her that no one else ever did, not even Patricia. Lynn struck a deal with the airline to purchase the in-house packaging company along with a silent partner. They planned to start a separate entity. She asked Patricia if she would come with her to the new company and help set up the group department. Patricia would be a consultant for Lynn's new company and be paid separately while still keeping her full-time job at the airline. Patricia was beside herself. No one had ever noticed her capabilities before, and she had never been considered for such high-level work. Patricia happily agreed and moonlighted for six months before Lynn offered her a full-time position. She would be running the department, implementing procedures, and streamlining costs.

Insecurity crept in. Patricia was a creature of comfort, and the complacency she felt at the airline was like a safety blanket. She had been there for over a decade, and the idea of change was terrifying. *What if I fail?* She always doubted her abilities and self-sabotaged. She knew staying at the airline was a dead-end job and had no growth potential. She would have to push herself in order to break out of her comfort zone. She decided to accept this new challenge. It was a once-in-a-lifetime opportunity.

Lynn was very generous with Patricia, taking an interest in teaching and mentoring her. As an additional bonus, the compensation and benefits were beyond anything Patricia could have ever imagined. Patricia was vested and took her job seriously, not wanting to let Lynn down. The revenue from the department she was running surpassed all the income from individual reservations. Her primary responsibilities consisted of negotiations and planning. These were two things she excelled at doing.

As the company was growing, a position became available for an executive salesperson. The person hired for the job would work directly with Lynn. There was an announcement in the paper and the breakroom. Patricia wanted the job, and she went to Lynn and told her.

"You'll have to apply just like everyone else," Lynn told her. "There is one other internal person who is also interested, and he has sales experience," Lynn continued without looking up from her desk. It was demotivating to hear, but Patricia was not going to give up, having learned that she couldn't wait around for it to happen if she wanted something. She had taken the first step by asking for it and making herself noticed.

Patricia interviewed for the job. And, as luck would have it, another job was posted that the other candidate wanted even more. She now had no competition in the candidate pool, and she secured the position for herself. She was beyond elated. Finally, she had her own office with a view and was now considered part of management. Patricia had visualized it, and there it was.

CHAPTER 23

The Setback

Patricia had a great job making more money than she thought possible, and a mentor who was teaching her more than she could have ever learned in school.

Her relationship with her family was progressing. She had set boundaries and stuck to them. Tony was doing well for himself. He was running and growing his own business with two other partners. Like Patricia, Tony was not dating and had a hard time curating healthy relationships. He had a son at the age of eighteen but never married his son's mother.

Maria continued living through her children and never remarried or made a life for herself. She dated one man who was going nowhere, a loser with no ambition. Even though he was affectionate to her, they argued all the time. He did not like working, and did not like Elizabeth, who was still living at home, making matters even more complicated.

Maria was always controlling, and with no one else around, she latched on to her youngest daughter. It did not leave much time for anything else, so her boyfriend eventually moved on.

Elizabeth was brilliant. She was top of her class and self-driven. Now a senior in high school, Tony did a great job mentoring her to make sure she would get into a good college. He was a father figure and watched over her.

Graduation was around the corner, and everyone was very proud of Elizabeth's achievements. She would be the first person in their family to graduate with honors and have a real chance of experiencing an authentic college experience. During all those years, Elizabeth still had a relationship with her father. She was the only one. Preparing for her high school graduation, Maria and Elizabeth were sending invitations, but there was a big question mark about Antonio attending. Not wanting to upset him, Elizabeth struggled with the decision of inviting him or not. She knew that no one wanted him there, but she did not want to make the call. Finally, she rolled the dice, simply leaving it to him, hoping he would not show up.

Unfortunately, he did. He was too much of a narcissist not to. He wanted to be seen and take credit for Elizabeth's success in school. Maria, Tony, and Patricia all sat together. The graduation was in a large stadium. None of them were aware that Antonio was there. When the graduation ended, Maria, Patricia, and Tony made their way up the ramp to meet Elizabeth. They had no idea that Antonio was doing the same thing from the other corner of the auditorium.

Patricia walked proudly with flowers in her hand toward Elizabeth. As she got closer, Patricia saw Antonio. He had not changed much since the last time she had seen him. Antonio walked rapidly with a stern look on his face, his chest proud and head held high. Patricia recognized his walk, and as her eyes made their way to his face, her breathing became rapid; she was in a cold sweat, and her heart was racing. Tony saw Patricia from the corner of his eye. Suddenly he saw her drop to the floor, curl up into a ball using a pillar for support, and crying hysterically. The flowers scattered on the floor as Patricia became child-like again. Tony backtracked and tried to pry her shaking body from the floor.

Elizabeth saw what was happening and ran to Antonio, asking him to leave immediately.

"What is wrong with her?" he yelled as he pitifully looked at Patricia.

"Just go!" Elizabeth repeated. With nothing else to do, he turned and walked away. A flood of emotions had taken over Patricia. She had not seen her father in eight years, and the mere sight of Antonio caused her to regress. Patricia was scared and insecure and felt shame and embarrassment for ruining Elizabeth's graduation.

They collected Patricia from the floor and waited for her to calm down. They assured her that Antonio had left the stadium and had nothing to worry about over the affair. The four of them walked out with Elizabeth in her graduation gown, looking back at everyone celebrating. When they made it back to Maria's house, Tony tried to talk to Patricia and ask her what had happened, but Patricia was still not ready to talk.

Elizabeth decided there was not much for her to do and left to celebrate with her friends, but before leaving, the phone rang, and it was Antonio. "What's wrong with your sister?" he asked. "She looked like she saw a ghost."

Elizabeth, unsure of what to answer, simply said, "You'd have to ask her."

"She is just as crazy as your mother," was Antonio's reply as he hung up the phone.

After Elizabeth left, Maria took Patricia to get the car she had left at the stadium. There was silence. Patricia finally spoke, only to apologize for ruining her sister's graduation. "I don't know what came over me, but I'm sorry."

Maria did not know what to say but utter, "Is it something I did? I did my best."

"No, mom, it's not about you," Patricia answered in frustration. *Even during a moment like this, she shows no empathy.*

A couple of days went by, and Patricia could not get the image of her father out of her head. She could not understand why she had such a strong reaction just by seeing him. How could someone have such control over her, with their mere presence?

Elizabeth called to express her sadness over the situation. "I wish I would have never invited him." Patricia pleaded with her not to take responsibility, as no one could have predicted the outcome. No sooner had she hung up with Elizabeth, when Tony called to see if there was anything he could do. Just then, it hit her that both her brother and her sister were concerned, asking what they could do, but neither of her parents showed much interest, and just like that, Patricia began to feel angry. They were the reason for her sadness and the emotional roller-coaster she was constantly riding.

Patricia started to get depressed and began to call in sick to work and started having the recurring dream again, only this time she wasn't able to get up from bed. She began to drink heavily and felt herself going down a destructive path once again.

Lynn started to notice Patricia's coming in late and lack of enthusiasm. "Is everything okay?" asked Lynn on more than one occasion. Lynn was compassionate until Patricia missed two major meetings, and then Lynn gave Patricia a warning. "I don't know what's going on, but this behavior is not acceptable." Patricia was in jeopardy of losing her job. She needed to get help and get it quickly. She had come too far in her life to go backward.

Patricia went back to the materials she had gotten from the hospital and started running again. Exercise would help give her the needed boost to get through the day.

Her actions were a patch, but it was unsatisfying knowing she was barely surviving. Luckily, her job started taking her on out-of-town trips, and it was a good distraction. On the downside, she would go out alone on these trips, drink, hang out with strangers, and often blackout. She must have had someone watching over her to avoid any serious damage.

After a four-day trip, Patricia returned from a conference and stopped by the office to drop off some things. She found Lynn distraught. Lynn was in her office, sobbing, and told Patricia that she was going through a divorce. Lynn needed Patricia to be on top of things now more than ever. *A tall order of me right now*, thought Patricia, but she knew she needed to step up and help Lynn. Lynn also knew it was a lot to ask of Patricia but felt that if Patricia had something to work for, it would give her a purpose. "I ask two things of you," Lynn explained. "Finish school—the company will pay for it—and talk to a therapist."

Lynn was clueless as to where Patricia's erratic behavior stemmed from, but she knew that Patricia needed help.

Finishing school was doable. The second task was more complicated. Patricia did not want to disappoint the one person who believed in her, so she abided. She registered for the next semester of school and looked for a therapist. It took three therapists before finding one that made her feel comfortable. She did not want to begin from zero and re-tell every traumatic experience of her life to a new therapist. So, she stuck with the present issues of dealing with stress and disappointments. It was a Band-Aid to get her through the hump.

Lynn was staying at the office later and later. She would ask Patricia to remain as well. Patricia focused on marketing and public relations for the international and national markets, which she enjoyed. The work kept her busy, distracted, and out of trouble. Lynn started relying more and more on Patricia at work and as a companion, someone to hang out with outside of the office. She introduced her to fine dining establishments and showed her how to order and eat with greater etiquette—the type of manners befitting a refined woman. Lynn had high-class dignity, coming from an old, wealthy Texas family.

Things started to get a little uncomfortable when Patricia began dating again. She had met a man in class whom she would occasionally go out and have dinner with. They always had a good time, but it left no time for Lynn. Lynn would get upset with Patricia and not talk to her. But then they would go on a business trip to New York or Miami or Mexico, and they'd work together, and all would be fine again between them. But Patricia started to worry about Lynn's reactions when she was not available. The relationship began to feel like her childhood, trapped when her mother would force her to stay home and act as her companion. It did not sit well with Patricia.

Patricia began to distance herself without saying anything or letting Lynn know how she felt. It was easier to disappear than be confrontational. Luckily for Patricia, Lynn's assistant was now going through a divorce and started depending on Lynn for stability, taking pressure off her.

On the home front, Elizabeth was at college, and Maria's codependency followed her there. She would visit Elizabeth every chance she got. Observing this behavior was extremely painful for Patricia.

Throughout the years, Patricia remained friends with Hope and her husband, and a couple of other people she had met at work. But she always found herself in compromising situations with the boyfriends and husbands of her friends. These men always seemed to come on to Patricia. She always assumed she was just being friendly with them, not flirtatious. One friend's boyfriend had tried to kiss her one night. When she told her friend this, the woman accused Patricia of lying and being jealous. After that encounter, whenever she felt an already-taken man was coming on to her, Patrica just pushed it aside and didn't broach the subject, often distancing herself from those people.

Men would come on to her aggressively at work as well. Patricia was always perplexed, feeling like she had a target on her back. She was attractive and fit, with long, black, curly hair and big black eyes. But there were plenty of pretty girls at work; none of them seemed to get the attention that she got. Patricia never considered herself to be beautiful. In her mind, she was always ugly and overweight. But men would try to take advantage of her. She wore the cloak of victimhood, coming across as being insecure. Some of these men felt they had power over her. She needed to find her power.

DAMAGED GOODS

Someone once told me I was damaged goods.

Yes, put together by broken soles.

I dug deep, found the energy to fuse my spirit, opened
my mind, and grasped at the universe. Crawling,
scratching, creating a work of art

I became a power to be reckoned with

I am not damaged. I am a reflection of all. I am a survivor.
I live, I love. Do not silence me

I will not be put down

Hear me, embrace me, look at me.

I am your sister, your neighbor, your wife, your friend.

CHAPTER 24

To Live or Not to Live

Work was crazy busy. Patricia was constantly feeling guilty about everything she did or said. She could not let go of the insecurities that had plagued her since childhood.

Patricia had to fly out of the country with some clients. Thankful for the distraction, she focused on her work. The trip was to Honduras, and a rafting and hiking excursion was on the agenda. On the hike day, the weather could not have been better. She was taking it all in, the nature, the breeze, and even the company of the people she was around.

The vibrant greens of the mountains served as the backdrop for the cascading waterfalls. The rays of sunlight bounced off the river, creating a rainbow of colors. The views were spectacular. At the end of the hike, there was a natural pool from the runoff of the river. Everyone jumped in. The area reminded Patricia of the image she would escape to as a child. She drifted away in thought.

"Jump in!" One of the guides was encouraging everyone to take a dive. Patricia hesitated, still frightened of the water. Patricia recalled the swim lessons her parents made her take after the first drowning incident, how hard it was for her to get in the water then, and how she excelled and enjoyed them afterward. She even went so far as to join the swim team at the Y and made the dive team. Jumping into a 12-foot pool without fear was an accomplishment.

Patricia sat at the bank of the river staring at the water and listening to the waterfall in the background as she listened to everyone laughing and having fun. It was a contradiction in her mind; she was terrified of water, yet it was also the most peaceful image she could conjure up. But just as she was about to jump, her mind immediately went back to her first drowning incident, and then she recalled her father pulling her out of the water and yelling at her. Her thoughts of wanting to stay at the bottom of the pool surged. Becky came back into her head, and she fast-forwarded to her sister's graduation, seeing herself curled up in a ball, rocking. She flashed to her guardian angel and how it was always present in her time of need. Her breath was out of control, and her mind was jumping from one scene to another. Patricia remembered what her therapist would say, "Enjoy and let go." *Enough!* She jumped in the river.

The river was deep, but she managed to swim and resurface as she headed towards the center of the watering hole. The further Patricia got from the edge, the more she could feel her body tensing until she could no longer move. Her breathing began to speed up as she started hyperventilating. Her body started to sink, and her mind drifted. Finally, closing her eyes, Patricia gave in to her falling body. It was almost as if she was calling it quits. The guide saw her sinking and rushed to her rescue.

"I thought you could swim," the guide said as he yanked her out of the water.

"I can. I just froze." *The third time's a charm*, she thought. *Could the first therapist be right? Was she a danger to herself? Was she subconsciously trying to end her life?*

Back at the lodge, Patricia sat on the deck in a trance. She recalled being alone in the car and driving as fast as she could while in a daze. It felt good playing Russian roulette and seeing how far she could take things or endure pain. Regardless of her work, the ill feelings towards herself still lingered. She had a total lack of respect for her being. Even the people she dated, she put up with so much from them. She was following a pattern. All her relationships were destructive, with her as the common denominator.

Patricia realized there was one thing she had not done; she had not sat alone in her thoughts to make sense of her life. Patricia was constantly moving from one thing to another, sweeping away mishaps and setbacks and pretending like they did not happen; moving on to making things okay.

She had vacation time accumulated and decided to take a couple of days and go to the beach in Zihuatanejo, Mexico. Desperately needing a reset, along with some alone time and sun, she made arrangements and hopped on a flight two days later. Her itinerary consisted of hanging out by the pool and beach and journaling.

The resort was buzzing with people, but she kept to herself, reading and writing. Patricia would wake up early, run on the beach, eat breakfast, and head out to lay on the sand. Then, she'd eat dinner alone in her room and repeat the same schedule the next day. She never felt more at ease than when she was near the water; the crashing waves were hypnotizing, and she could spend hours staring at them. Again, her thoughts pondered over how a power of nature could instill so much fear when she physically engaged with it and provide so much peace when she merely gazed upon it.

After several days of journaling and processing the events back home, Patricia had a better grasp of her feelings and gained positive thoughts. She felt prepared to deal with the real world. Patricia said goodbye to the sun, sea, and the stars and packed for her return.

When her flight arrived in Houston, she became burdened with a heavy feeling but quickly focused on more positive thoughts. Before leaving Mexico, she had made a list of goals she wanted to achieve personally and professionally.

The next day while driving to work, the heavy burden she had felt the day before returned. She once again refocused her thoughts. But the moment she arrived, Lynn called her into her office. Her reception was not what she was expecting. Patricia anticipated Lynn asking questions about her trip and planned on telling her about the goals she had assigned to herself. Only Lynn's face had a different story to tell. She sat behind her desk with a grim look and a glass of whiskey. "I have a pressing matter to discuss with you," Lynn was extremely serious. "There have been a lot of changes since you've been gone, and we need to make some arrangements. The company sold, and my partners from New York are coming in to sign the paperwork this week."

"I knew nothing," Patricia was in total shock.

"I've had to keep it a secret as it's a huge negotiation." Patricia wondered what would happen but did not want to pry or push for more information. Lynn looked stressed, and Patricia didn't want to put her insecurities on Lynn. But she immediately thought of the future. *What am I going to do? Am I ready for a change?*

Before she knew it, the New York partners were there and signing the paperwork. Everyone was given three months notice to find new jobs, and Patricia went into panic mode. Everything was happening so fast. Not sure what to do, she finally confided in Lynn, told her how she felt, and asked for help. "I'm happy to help however I can."

She graciously called a friend on the hotel side and got her an interview. Patricia knew Lynn's friend, having met him once at a luncheon; she was not a fan. He had a grandiose personality and an even bigger mouth. She recalled that he spoke badly about everyone he knew during lunch and demanded things be served to him immediately. Lynn had even nicknamed him "The Great One."

That night, Patricia went to dinner with Hope to catch up and tell her everything that had happened. During dinner, they observed someone passing by them, back and forth, numerous times. *What is going on*, she wondered. The man finally approached them.

"My name is Art," he said. "Would yall like to go for a drink?" Patricia politely declined, but Hope was game.

"Let's go!" Hope said. "What can it hurt?" Hope was like that, very spontaneous, but it was the furthest thing from Patricia's mind. She wanted no part of men.

Art was a good-looking guy in his mid-20s, wearing an expensive suit and tie which matched his light brown hair and hazel eyes. He had a frat boy look about him. Art grabbed each of their hands and led them across the street. Patricia reluctantly followed; something about him made her radar go off. They ended up at a swanky bar to have a drink. Art got them both a glass of wine and proceeded to school them, "I saw that trash wine you were drinking. You should make better choices." Patricia did not find his comment funny or clever in any way. She immediately got up and threw the glass of wine into a nearby planter and called to Hope so they could leave. Unfortunately, Hope was not ready to end the night and insisted they drive Art home. Hope found out his friends had left him in conversation, and he needed a ride.

Patricia drove as Hope and Art sat in the back seat. He was very chatty and talked about his family. It was hard to tell who he was interested in as he was very flirtatious with both of them. They finally arrived at his apartment and let him out. When they got him home, he insisted on them coming up to have a drink with him, but Patricia quickly declined and left before Hope could say another word.

The next day, Lynn's friend, Sam, called Patricia. There was a job opening, and he wanted to talk to her. "An informal interview," he said. Patricia paused for a moment on the phone and told him she was not looking for a job in the hotel industry.

"Just come in, and we can talk about your future. I have lots of contacts and can help you get to where you want to be."

Patricia agreed and went to meet with him the next day. True to his reputation, Sam was late. According to the rumors, he felt that his time was more valuable than anyone else's and he was worth waiting for. When she walked into the office, the receptionist at the front desk seemed to be manning phones, taking messages, doing paperwork, and juggling what seemed like the job of 20 people.

"I thought this was a big operation with a lot of people," quipped Patricia.

"They all walked out," answered the poor woman. "And I'm next." She was about to get up and leave when Sam walked in.

"Darling, come in, have a seat in my office, and close the door, won't you?" Sam was a heavy man with a shiny, bald head, wearing a suit with no jacket. He looked Middle Eastern but had a Spanish accent.

"Tell me what you are going to do with your life." Before Patricia could open her mouth to respond, he continued talking.

"That hair! Are you going to cut it? It's big. We can get you a new look. Anyway, tell me." Once again, she attempted to talk, but once again, he interrupted her. "Do you always dress that way?"

Patricia ignored him.

"I'd like to find a job with an airline."

"No, no, no, you don't want to do that. Airlines are the past; you need to focus on hotels." Patricia was confused. *Why am I here?* Sam continued, "Look, I'll make a deal with you if you come to work for me for three months. I'll get you an interview with American Airlines. They are all my friends."

"What happened to all your staff?" she asked.

"When people work for me, they automatically get jobs at the most prestigious firms. They have all moved on. You know, people are just so ungrateful. They have no loyalty." Attempting to convince her, Sam went on to tell her about the position and the direction he envisioned the company heading in with the right person. He was trying to make the work seem more interesting than it was in reality.

"You'll be handling all the marketing activities worldwide for luxury hotels and several other clients we promote. You'll also travel all around the world and stay at the best hotels. I bet you've never done that before." It sounded exciting, but she had her doubts. It seemed too good to be true, and the office seemed a mess. Not to mention, Sam's personality was a lot to take.

After talking endlessly, he finally wore Patricia down, and she agreed to work for him for three months and only three months. Patricia went back and told Lynn about her conversation with Sam. Lynn offered her the opportunity to take her three-month notice and work with Sam, and she would continue paying her.

"There is not much else to do here," she said. Patricia thanked her and agreed to the plan.

It was a sad moment for Patricia as Lynn was more than just an employer for her; she was a mentor and a friend. Patricia recognized that Lynn was the only person in her life that took the time to teach her and groom her for a better future.

Before Patricia left, Lynn confessed that her New York partners were trying to sell the company from under her. She could see that Lynn was in dire straits. Lynn was a kind and generous person who did not deserve the treatment she got. Towards the end, she salvaged some of her money, but not what she deserved. Her father had to come in and rescue her. Lynn was a proud woman, so she never divulged any of the information from the business transaction. Ultimately, the company was sold to what would become The Expedia Group.

Soon after the acquisition, Lynn retired and she and Patricia lost touch. However, Patricia always felt a debt to Lynn for her generosity. She had taken Patricia under her wing and believed in her abilities. Patricia hoped one day to see her again and be able to thank her. She vowed to pay it forward, helping others along the way.

CHAPTER 25

New Era and Old Acquaintances

A few days before starting her new job, she got a call.

"Hey, it's Art. What are you up to? Do you want to have dinner tonight?"

"Art, who?" Patricia had no recollection of anyone named Art.

"The guy you and your friend gave a ride to." *Oh, that guy!*

"How'd you get my number?" asked Patricia.

"You left it in my coat pocket."

"Ahh, no." She definitely remembered that she did NOT leave her number in his pocket.

Hope, I'm going to kill her.

"Anyway, do you want to have dinner tonight? There's a great restaurant I've wanted to try."

"Sure, okay." *So what do I have to lose?*

"I'll pick you up at seven. What's your address?"

Art picked up Patricia in a thoroughly detailed Jeep. For a first date, they had a great time. Patricia had never gone out with someone like Art. He was intelligent, witty, and spontaneous. This caught Patricia completely off guard. His behavior was different from the first time she met him. She instantly went from total dislike to admiring Art. *I misjudged him.* His charm was more than she could resist. Not at all what she expected.

After dinner, they went to a jazz bar for drinks, and he took her home. She knew she needed to do this right. She could not get too needy and run him off. She had to play it cool. They hung out again the next day and then again for the next three days.

At the time, Art's dad lived with him. He was helping his dad change careers and was training him in computer science. *What a great son*, she thought. Art was constantly working, in the middle of the night, between workouts, and during dinner.

"That's my world," he would say. They were together for several days, and then Patricia would not hear from him for a couple of days. Then, out of the blue, Art would call her to say he was going out with friends and invite her to join. So, she did. They drank a lot and laughed a lot. Patricia nicknamed him "the king of the nerds." All his friends were brilliant but had no personalities. Art had a big personality and was probably the most intelligent of the group. Art caught Patricia off guard. His dad was a plus. She spent hours talking to him while Art worked. Patricia felt comfortable around both of them. One night during dinner, Art's dad, with a smirk on his face, asked Patricia, "How's the Jeep holding up? Is it still clean?" Patricia looked at him, confused. "It's not as clean as when I first met Art, but it's okay." "You know I had it detailed for his first date with you." Art's dad continued. "No, I was not aware," Patricia replied. By now, Patricia was not surprised—she had come to know Art a little better and realized his dad cared for most things for him.

Meanwhile, Patricia started working with Sam, and it was chaos. There were no files, no instructions, and she had no clue what to do.

The same woman that was there during her interview was still there. She threw a bunch of files on Patricia's desk.

"You need to organize an event for these hoteliers next month. There is a manual somewhere on how to do it."

Sam rarely came into the office, so Patricia took things into her own hands without asking. She was fielding calls from people asking about the event. Somehow, she managed to piece things together with the small amount of information given. Finally, the night before the event, Sam came to the office to ask if everything was ready.

"Yes," Patricia proudly proclaimed.

"Let me see what you have put together." He reviewed the plan and, without asking questions, went into a rage. "This is not how we do it! It is your last day if things fail tomorrow." Patricia was confused. He gave her no direction but claimed that things were wrong. *Not a good start*, she thought.

The event went better than expected, and people complimented her on a job well done. Except for Sam, he was upset with her. He did not like that she had changed things around. No one dared to challenge Sam.

The three months passed by quickly, and there was no mention of his promise to her to help with a different job. Her compensation was half of what she was receiving with Lynn, and every time Patricia would bring it up to Sam, he would put her off. However, she was learning a lot, so she did not press the issue. Instead, she took ownership of the position and felt it was a worthwhile investment for a little longer.

By now, it had been a while since she had seen Maria. It was time to reach out and check in on her. They went to lunch and caught up on the family drama. There was always drama. Antonio had lost his home and was about to lose his business. The drinking had gotten the best of him, and he was living in his car. Jen was sending Marlo, their daughter, to visit Antonio, and she would stay in the car with him. Not the wisest decision.

Maria also went on to tell her that her Uncle Juan had reached out to her. So much time had gone by since they spoke about him.

"Why would he call you?" asked Patricia.

"They are living in Canada," continued Maria. "They had to flee during the civil war in El Salvador," Juan told her that he had been kidnapped and forced to drive around, putting bombs in buildings. After the incident, he sought asylum.

"That's terrible," Patricia replied with a blank look on her face. She felt nothing and was not interested in what was happening with him and his family.

"There is more." Maria went on to tell her that Carlos had confessed to what he had done to her. Patricia just stared at her, wondering what else was going to come out of her mouth. "Right before Carlos married Patty, he went to talk to Juan and apologized for what he had done. He confessed." Maria said it with much excitement.

Patricia was not impressed, and she felt that it was too late. She had already survived that part of her life, and Carlos clearing his conscience was of no use to her. He could rot. She still had many scars from what he had done, and he got away with it in the end. His confession was for him to ease his own guilt; it did nothing for Patricia. *She* still had to live with the pain, shame, and anger of a rape. His actions had destroyed her relationship with Uncle Juan, the only person she had felt love from as a child. In her Uncle Juan's eyes, she felt that she would always be considered a liar.

Their lunch had left Patricia exhausted, and she went home to take a nap. But, when she woke up, instead of feeling rested, she felt uneasy. After all the time that had passed, and all the therapy, any mention of things from her childhood would put her on edge. Patricia desperately just wanted those memories and events to be gone from her life. She felt like she had already lived a thousand lifetimes, and all those memories seemed to belong to someone else, like she was watching them unfold from afar.

CHAPTER 26

Finding Your Voice

Things should have been going great with a new job and a new boyfriend. But the reality was that her new job seemed temporary and had no structure. Her new boyfriend seemed the same. Patricia craved stability, and she needed to feel secure.

Art was very inconsistent, calling Patricia occasionally and asking her out at the last minute. At first, it seemed fun that he was spontaneous, but the relationship never progressed. He would often make plans with her and then forget. Sometimes, she would go days without hearing from him. Patricia had become fond of him, but the lack of communication made her feel insecure, forcing her to ask questions, which pushed Art away.

Patricia did not pursue other relationships and found herself with little or no friends. She waited around for Art to call, only to be disappointed when he did not make her the priority. Art liked going out with people after work, and Patricia began to feel like she was a second choice.

Throughout her entire life, others had dictated the outcome of things for Patricia. Now she was ready to take things into her own hands. Knowing she had been doing a great job at work and taking on additional responsibilities, she called a meeting with Sam and gave him an ultimatum. Patricia reminded Sam of the promises he had made to her and the conditions he agreed to when she came to work for him. He needed to give her a raise, more autonomy, and put a structure in place—or she would leave. He did not agree right away and told her he needed to think about it.

Patricia confronted Art and told him she needed the relationship to progress. His response was not something she was expecting. Art informed her he was moving to Costa Rica to work at a startup. Just like that, he was gone.

Sam spent weeks out of the office. When he finally returned, he called her in and told her he was sick. He had been diagnosed with cancer, and he needed her to take over all his future trips and responsibilities until he returned from treatment. It was not what she had planned when she had hoped to move forward. Patricia now felt responsible for Sam's work; she even felt responsible for Sam. She still had not realized that she could control things for herself without letting the external scenarios dictate her actions.

Patricia had to prepare, physically and mentally. She inherited a heavy travel schedule through Europe and North America. She was nervous as some of Sam's stops included speaking engagements in front of hundreds of people; this was not something she was comfortable doing.

While she was packing, the phone rang.

"Do you know Antonio Lopez?"

"Yes," she replied.

"He is missing, and we are trying to find him."

"I have not seen him in ages." Not wanting to continue with the questioning, she hung up the phone. She felt cold and unsteady, but she did not have time to deal with anything relating to Antonio. Whatever the call was about, she wanted no part of it.

The next day she was leaving for Berlin, Germany—her first stop on the agenda. Patricia was excited and scared. She was attending a major networking event where people came to negotiate contracts and close deals. With no formal instructions, Patricia got on a plane and landed in Frankfurt, where she had to take a train to Berlin.

Patricia had never been to Germany, nor did she speak German. Overwhelmed and confused, she got off the plane to look for the train. Customs stopped her, and they motioned for her to show them her computer. After an hour of going through her things, they let her proceed. By then, she had missed her connecting train. Patricia could not afford a delay as the event was the following day.

She walked through the terminal as people rushed by. There were rows and rows of departure platforms, each with trains coming and going. Patricia attempted to purchase a new train ticket, but the language barrier and the fact that she felt like a fish out of water were not helping. Finally, someone saw how confused she was and helped her get where she needed to go. Thankful for the stranger's help, she boarded the train and made her way.

Patricia attended a few meetings the next day, but the buyers she met with were skeptical when they saw that she was not Sam. Somehow, she overcame the initial adverse reaction and closed the deals anyway. She had to transform herself into a positive, self-assured go-getter. It took all her energy and creativity. When the day was over, she was exhausted, mainly from the mental stress of being someone she wasn't. Being social and putting herself out there was not something she embraced. She still had two more days of meetings and two weeks' worth of trips. Patricia knew she would have to dig deep to find the confidence she needed to complete her mission.

On the east side of Berlin, a cocktail party for the conference was taking place. The venue was in a small boutique hotel that had just opened that week. The party had a club vibe with a DJ playing house music, dimly lit areas, and a bar on every floor. She arrived alone, so she immediately started to look around the room for people she recognized. She spotted someone she once worked with and approached him with much enthusiasm. She felt out of place and nervous, so seeing someone familiar gave her comfort. She and Tim hung out for a while, and he introduced her to several people. One group of Berliners stuck close to her. Fashionably dressed and statuesque, they towered her.

The drinks never stopped flowing, and she began to let her guard down and relax. The alcohol helped her socialize, get out of her head, and have a good time. Then, sometime during the night, a drink was brought to her by one of the Berliners, and, before she knew it, she woke up in her hotel room the following day. She was still dressed from the night before, with her clothes in disarray. However, Patricia could not remember what had happened. She had flashes of being near a dock. *But how did I get into my hotel room?* The sunlight darting in from the window was blinding, and her brain was in a fog. She went downstairs to ask the front desk if they had seen anything the previous night. They simply said someone had brought her in. She had no time to continue wondering; she had to get dressed and get to the conference.

As Patricia was getting ready, the television was on in the background, and she could hear a sermon. It was Joel Osteen talking about being determined and enjoying life. "Only you can help yourself achieve happiness." *How ironic.* Joel Osteen was a famous preacher from Houston, and he was chanting words she had heard previously while in troubling situations.

She arrived at the conference and immediately looked for Tim, but he avoided her and claimed not to know anything about the night before when she pressed him for information. *Could I have been roofied?* Once again, she was taken off guard and became an easy target. Still perplexed as to why these circumstances kept happening to her, Patricia again blamed herself. It never crossed her mind that people saw her vulnerability as a target to take advantage of repeatedly. So, with no one to blame or even talk to and no evidence of what did or didn't happen the night before, Patricia kept silent.

Then she remembered the words she had heard earlier that day. So, she went back and talked to Tim, pressuring him to tell her what had happened. She needed to know.

"You left with the Berliners. You seemed fine when you left," he said.

"Then why all the silence?" Patricia was losing her patience.

"Look, I'm not here to get anyone in trouble. These guys were just looking to have fun, and you were an easy target." Tim finally told her where they worked. Not wanting to put herself in any more danger, she went to the local police and filed a report.

A couple of days later, Patricia had to continue her trip. She arrived at the airport, and as she was waiting for her plane, she picked up a local newspaper. To her surprise, the guys she had been with at the party were pictured in an article. She could not read German, so she asked a lady next to her what the article said. The lady read that the police had apprehended a group of men that were taking advantage of vulnerable out-of-town women. They were drugging the women, and their latest target was in the hospital, but the men's arrest was possible through a lead from one of the previous victims. It didn't erase what happened to her, but it would keep them from doing the same to someone else, which would have to be enough.

Patricia continued her trip. The second to last stop was New York City. Physically exhausted and mentally drained, she arrived at the hotel. She opened the door to her room, and sitting inside her room was Art. He was waiting for her. Somehow, the front desk had let him enter the room. She was happy to see him but also shocked. He was the last person she would have ever expected to see.

"How did you know I was here?" she asked.

"I called your office, and they told me. So I flew in from Costa Rica," he proudly said.

"You didn't call. I have not heard from you in months." Patricia remembered that she was upset with him and the way he had just left.

"I know. I'm sorry, but I'm here now." Patricia had a soft spot for him, and after all that had happened, she was happy to see him.

Art finished out the trip with her. With the final stop in Boston, they both returned to Houston. Patricia asked how long he would be staying, but Art was not one to give many answers. As a matter of fact, it bothered him to have to provide explanations. Finally, Patricia decided she'd go with it and leave things alone. She liked him a lot. His spontaneity was a draw, and his fearless attitude energized her.

CHAPTER 27

Lost and Not Found

When Patricia got back to the office, she had numerous missed calls and messages from the same man that had called her looking for Antonio. Not wanting to fall back into the past, she ignored them. Eventually, curiosity got the best of her, so Patricia called Maria to see if she knew anything or if she had heard something about Antonio. She told Maria a man had been calling her asking about her dad. Maria, in fact, was very informed and proceeded to tell her that Antonio had lost his business and fled the country with several of his customers' cars. Maria had learned this from his sister shortly after being questioned about his disappearance by an assumed detective.

The next time the man called Patricia, she answered. She was intrigued about why he wanted to talk to her.

"You are listed as his emergency contact," the detective informed Patricia. That was hard for her to believe.

"When was the last time you saw or heard from Antonio?" the man asked.

"I have not seen him in years," answered Patricia. "I have no idea where he is, and I have not talked to him." Patricia started to feel worried.

"We need to find him. He is in a lot of trouble." The man continued.

"He would never reach out to me," Patricia explained. "You should know that after talking to other people." Patricia began to get suspicious and went on to ask the questions she had for the detectives. "When was he seen last? Who was he with? What kind of trouble was he facing?"

"All questions we can't answer," said the detective. "If I hear anything, I'll call you." The detective hung up on her.

Antonio was a rotten person, not worthy of anyone's concerns, but she could not help but wonder if he was okay. *Was he somewhere dead? Why would he take someone's car?* She went over the questions in her mind many times until she could not stand it anymore and decided to do some digging of her own.

Patricia left work and drove to the shop he had leased for years, where she had worked with him. The gate had a lock with a sign that warned against trespassers and a phone number. She called the number and told them who she was. She went on to explain she was looking for information on her father. The man on the other line was the property owner's son. He informed her that his father had passed away a couple of years ago and that, before he passed, they had offered to sell Antonio the property for a mere fraction of its actual worth. He rejected the offer, claiming he did not have the money. He left during the night, skipping out on the rent, and they had not heard anything from him.

She walked around the neighborhood where the shop was and went into the restaurants Antonio would frequent. *Everyone knew him.*

Someone must know something, she thought. Finally, Patricia went into Mel's BBQ joint on the corner. The owner informed her that Antonio had been acting strange the weeks preceding his disappearance, and they would often have to call one of his buddies to take him home.

"It wasn't one of his normal binge drinking modes," the man said. "It was like he had lost all sense of where he was." Patricia thanked him and left. She went to the store down the street where he would purchase beer. There, they told her that they had not seen him in a while but had heard rumors he had some strange guys hanging around the shop.

At this point, Patricia decided to head toward his old house. It was just a couple of miles from the shop. The door had boards on it with an eviction notice. She walked around the house and found a side door that was open. Her heart was racing, unsure of what she was going to find inside. She made her way into the ransacked living room. *Someone had been looking for something, but what? Someone must know something*, She thought.

Patricia remembered the office manager, Steve. She went home and looked him up. Antonio had taken him in after a bad motorcycle accident. She found his number and called him. The two agreed to meet the next day at 1:00 p.m. She had only seen the guy once, which was also the last time she had been at her father's shop. They met at a coffee shop near the auto repair. Patricia filled Steve in on the information the detective had given her. Steve was caught entirely off guard by the meeting. She asked if he had any information.

"He had started to do some odd business dealings with one of his neighbors across the street, who was a narcotics agent," Steve began to tell her reluctantly. "I can't go into too much detail as I was not privy to anything, but there were a lot of packages coming and going."

"What kind of packages?" asked Patricia.

"Not sure," he shrugged his shoulders. "I left shortly after it all started. I was feeling uncomfortable."

"What was the name of the neighbor?" she asked. His name was John, answered Steve, and her heart skipped a beat. It was the same name as the detective that had been calling her.

Things were now starting to make sense. Antonio must have gotten in over his head with the detective and fled to avoid trouble. Patricia wondered about her half-sister, Marlo, and her whereabouts and hoped she was not around during this time in their father's life. Her concerns led her to call Jen in Philadelphia and to ask if she knew anything about Antonio. Jen told Patricia she had heard from him recently and that he was in Guatemala. He had taken one of the cars and was hiding out until everything blew over. Patricia was surprised that Jen was so forthcoming. But Jen was also angry at him. Jen went on to tell her, "Antonio stopped paying child support and has not checked in on us in months. I'm struggling to make ends meet while apparently he is shacked up with some woman in Guatemala who is supposedly having his child."

Patricia said, "I'm sorry." It was the only words that seemed appropriate at the time. "My father has never been able to see past his own needs."

While the story Jen told seemed like a tall tale, she believed Jen. Even without confirming any of the information, they were all things Antonio was capable of doing.

Meanwhile, work needed her, and at that point, there was nothing else to do regarding Antonio. He had gotten himself into a mess he had created, and Patricia was sure he would somehow find a way to get out of it. She went back to work, hoping she could catch Sam. Unfortunately, no one had seen him in days, as he was going through chemo treatments. Patricia would have to wait for him to return so that she could figure out how she would get compensated.

Months went by with no sign of Sam. His friend, Nick, who had come in from Mexico to help around the office, would also assist with things around Sam's house. Patricia liked Nick. He was funny and made things enjoyable. His enthusiasm for living was contagious. Patricia confided in Nick and told him she would look for another job as soon as Sam returned. Nick must have told Sam because Sam showed up to work and called her in the office the next week. Not only did he offer Patricia a raise, but Sam also offered her a partnership in the company.

She was totally surprised. Sam needed Patricia. She had a dedication and drive that no one had and was a quick learner. Who else was going to resolve his issues? Sam had been gone for months, and Patricia forged forward, taking ownership. She possessed the qualities that he was lacking.

Giving her shares of the company offered Sam peace of mind that Patricia would not leave. He was very astute and knew she'd continue working harder now that she had ownership. Sam proceeded to have his lawyers draw up papers and make everything official.

CHAPTER 28

A Reflection of Gratitude

By now, Patricia and Art were living together. His work schedule took him to St. Louis during the week and back home to Houston on the weekends. She had the privilege of meeting the rest of Art's family, who lived on the lake about three hours from Houston. It was instant love when she met them. They were the picture of the perfect family, the kind seen on television. Even better, Patricia adored Art's mother. She had a great sense of humor, and everything seemed just to roll off her back. As a fifth-grade teacher and a mother to a man like Art, she needed to be that way. Art and his mother were close, making time to talk often. She was the only one that could give Art direction. His younger sister was in high school. She was gorgeous, athletic, intelligent, the head cheerleader, and involved in every sport. She was the exact opposite of what Patricia had been in high school.

Patricia also adored Art. She had never loved anyone the way she loved him. But he was not as expressive with his feelings, nor did he want a traditional relationship. A commitment was not top on his priority list. Instead, he was a free spirit who worked intensely. Art showed his affection in different ways. He pushed Patricia to do better, to reach further than she thought she could.

While Art and Patricia moved in together, Maria had gone to live with Tony. She sold their childhood house and moved in with him, waiting for Elizabeth to finish college. Maria held on to the hope that Elizabeth would come back and they'd move in together. Meanwhile, she was still making trips back and forth to see her in college.

Tony had never married, but lived with his girlfriend and had full-time custody of his son, who was born when Tony was 18. Maria added to that living situation was a recipe for disaster.

Carri, Tony's live-in girlfriend, was under constant scrutiny from Maria. Maria was constantly commenting on everything Carri did. "That woman does not know how to clean," she would profess. "What does she do all day?" was her favorite question to stir up trouble.

For the most part, Carri ignored Maria until Carri became pregnant. At that point, Maria had so many things to say about their living situation and how the child should be raised. Maria's behavior was that of a matriarch. She expected everyone to do what she said. Only, Carri had other plans for raising her child. She spoke to Tony and told him she could no longer tolerate his mother's undermining and he needed to choose between the two of them.

Tony asked Maria to leave, but there was one caveat that Maria always held over his head. Maria had given Tony the money for the down payment on the house. It was never clear whether it was a loan or if she intended to live with him full time. It became a nasty family feud, one that lasted over five years. Maria went so far as to hire a lawyer.

Maria moved out. In the meantime, Maria would tell anyone who would listen what she had to endure. Obviously, her narrative resonated with many people. She was an older woman with little resources being taken advantage of by her son; it gave her the spotlight she craved. As a result, Maria was able to get a lot of mileage from her ordeal, including sympathy from Patricia and Elizabeth, who both took their mother's side and did not speak to Tony. Tony's sons, who were stripped of a relationship from their paternal side, were the real victims. They were the casualties of the unfounded war waged between mother and son.

No one could see how Maria liked controlling the family dynamics. She had the power to make everyone dislike one another, making her both the victim and the good woman. It was a destructive game that she played with everyone. They had never been a close family, but Maria's actions were now driving them farther apart.

With everything going on, Patricia attached herself to Art's family. Like a boat lost at sea, she floated around looking for a home. Patricia was desperate to live a happy life. She continued therapy and would change therapists depending on what she wanted to work on, learning that not all therapists were the right fit for everyone. As a result, mental clarity was hard to achieve.

Back at the office, Sam worked his "full-time" hours, which meant being in the office once or twice a week and traveling to exotic destinations the rest of the time. Patricia had grown to love Sam, seeing him as a father figure. Her respect for him was second to none. He was a mentor to Patricia and had taught her how to develop her creativeness. However, he was still very critical of her, especially her looks. Patricia was not one for makeup or looking extravagant. Sam loved anyone who was overdone and stood out in a crowd. All Patricia ever wanted to do was hide in the crowd.

Sam had become dependent on Patricia to run the office, including creating his reports for client meetings. Her need to please him and have him recognize the work she was doing overshadowed everything. Patricia never believed in herself. If she had, she would have recognized his selfish behavior.

Patricia had a friend that worked for a local talk show. They were looking for guests to talk about health and wellness destinations. One of her clients was a famous spa in Thailand, so her friend reached out and asked Patricia to come on the show. She was nervous and, at first, did not think she would be the right person.

"Let me see if Sam will be around," was her response when first asked. Then she thought about it and decided she needed to do it.

Nervous, Patricia went on the show as an expert, though she did not feel like an expert about anything. She only saw herself as an over-weight little girl who was useless at everything. The interview went off without a hitch, and Patricia came across as smart and approach-able, with an abundance of knowledge. Everyone loved her except Sam. He was upset that Patricia had taken the spotlight away from him. But his disappointment was short-lived. Patricia's appearance on the show had brought the company more exposure, and she was able to secure more clients. So Sam had nothing to complain about after all.

A couple of weeks after the interview, Sam attended a client meeting in Thailand, and the highlight of his presentation was the interview Patricia had hosted. Sam took full credit for setting up the interview and procuring exposure on a national television show. Not once did he give Patricia credit for her achievement.

Patricia noticed the similarities between Sam and Maria. They both demanded large amounts of attention, lacked empathy, and wanted to control everything. She needed a break from both of them and decided a vacation was a great idea. Nick, Sam's friend, was hosting a Mexican festival in Greece. She jumped at the opportunity to go and meet him. It was the middle of summer and a great time to get out of dodge before the busy fall season started.

When Art found out about her plans, he asked if he could come with her. Patricia always wanted him to join her, but he was usually never available, so she had stopped even bothering to ask. But this time, he was just as excited as she was, so they set out for a two-week vacation that turned into a month. It was more than she could have ever hoped. They were on the island of Santorini with turquoise blue backgrounds. There, everything was simple, quaint, and authentic. Nothing was mass-produced or commercial. Everyone on the island knew Nick, so they were treated like locals, not tourists. The experience made her grateful for all her achievements. She realized that she had not had her recurring dreams in a long time. Her life was stable, and the need to be watched over did not seem as important as it had been before. She was living in gratitude, a place she never imagined she would be.

CHAPTER 29

History Repeats

Patricia was ready for the next chapter in her life. For her, this meant having a family. Art was still reluctant and dismissed the idea. She feared being alone more than she feared not having her dreams of having children fulfilled. She decided not to discuss the issue with Art any further. He was not capable of listening and would dismiss any feeling she had. Art insisted on not recognizing feelings; he proclaimed to only react to facts. Feelings were abstract.

Patricia confided in her friends, and they all said to give him an ultimatum. But she was not about ultimatums; people needed to do things because they wanted to in the end.

A client offered to give her a dog. It was a perfect distraction and would help Patricia with her need to expand her family. The only issue was that the dog was in Mexico City. The puppy was part of a litter bred from championship dogs, and all the pups were in high demand.

She was nervous about flying to Mexico to get a dog, but knowing someone else might get it before she got the chance, she bought a return flight for the same day and boarded a plane. Patricia was picked up from the airport and driven to the breeder's home. There were ten puppies in the litter, and she could pick any one she wanted.

One playful puppy caught her eye. He ran up to her and sniffed her, then ran off again. This game continued for a while. She observed all the puppies, but it was the first one who kept coming back to her. *Meant to be*, she thought.

"It's this one," she said to the breeder. She packed him up and headed back to the airport. It was love at first sight.

"I'll name him Chilango, Chili for short," she announced to Art when she got home. "Chilango is slang for people from Mexico City," she went on to explain. He was a black Newfoundland Labrador with a small brown spot on his left rear side. A handsome dog, Art fell for him just as quickly as Patricia had.

Chili went everywhere with Patricia, including to work. He even slept in bed with her as her warmth tempered his puppy whimpers.

Patricia thought of the pets they had as children. Those animals had never been treated like they were family. Instead, they were used and abused. Her desire to change this manifested in her adoration for Chili. At the same time, it made her reflect on how her parents had treated their family, their children. They had also been used and abused. Patricia never wanted to do that to another human being. She started to doubt her ability to be a provider and caretaker. Maybe it was not a good idea to have children. After all, she had Art, a good job, and Chili. At least that's what she told herself to get past what she really wanted.

Her relationship with Maria had its ups and downs, at best. But she had created a bond with Elizabeth. The two got along well, and they had become friends. After college, Elizabeth procured a job in Houston and came home just as Maria wanted. Elizabeth, however, had plans of her own that did not include her mother. She fell for a guy at work, Armando. He was handsome, witty, charming, and dangerous. Armando came from an alcoholic background and stayed true to the disease himself. They moved in together, much to Maria's dismay. Maria was no longer living at Tony's but was engaged in a horrible legal battle with him.

Elizabeth had always dated men like Antonio, and her current boyfriend was no different. Patricia worried about her sister but knew there was nothing she could do about it. Elizabeth was a grown woman, intelligent, and capable of making her own decisions.

Armando never lacked friends or a social life. He and Elizabeth were always out partying, at bars or friends' houses. Armando could party all day and night. And, just like Antonio, when he got drunk, he would become offensive and say abusive things to Elizabeth. Elizabeth just took it. As a matter of fact, there was nothing she would not do for him.

One night, things had gotten more out of control than usual. Armando had been doing more than just drinking. Patricia was already home and in bed when she got a phone call from Maria, who was hysterical.

"He has smashed her face in," Maria was screaming. "He has lost his mind." Patricia listened but could not believe what she was hearing. She could barely get the words out of her mouth.

"Is she okay?"

"Elizabeth was able to get away and call me," replied Maria. "I drove over immediately and began alerting everyone." *It was surreal how this could be happening again.* They were all reliving what they had been through with Antonio.

After that episode, Armando and Elizabeth split for a little while. Armando took no responsibility for his actions, and Elizabeth disassociated from the situation and moved on as she was accustomed to as a child. Armando waited a couple of weeks, but soon enough, began to court Elizabeth back to him. He claimed to have no recollection of the night in question and swore it would never happen again.

Within no time, they were back together and engaged. Everyone warned Elizabeth it was the wrong thing to do, but she insisted that she loved him and that he loved her. She claimed that one night had been a mistake, she had set him off, and he would never do that again. The wedding was to take place in six months. During that time, many warning signs surfaced, but the marriage was to go on.

The situation made Patricia's anxiety rise again. Fearful and hopeless, her sister was heading in the same direction as her mother, and being unable to stop Elizabeth caused much despair. Patricia failed to understand how people continued to fall into the same pattern. Elizabeth was a highly educated woman with a support system and resources. As far as Patricia was concerned, these things only happened to poor people with no education or means, but this was not the case.

Abuse does not discriminate. It affects people from all walks of life, shapes, and colors. It only takes a simple formula to bring the abuser and the abused together. Elizabeth, a highly empathetic individual, was raised by two narcissistic parents. Armando, with a substance abuse problem and lacking ethics and empathy, was like a magnet for her.

Elizabeth had absorbed all of Maria's insecurities which, along with her lack of approval, sympathy, and praise, made her a target for men like Armando. It also made Patricia wonder what Elizabeth had seen or experienced when she visited Jen and Antonio when she was younger. She never talked about the visits to her father's home.

In need of relief to rid her anxiety, Patricia sought out yoga. According to many, it was the answer to relaxation and mental clarity. It was not something she had tried in the past as it seemed slow. She preferred a faster-paced workout. But her desperate need for peace of mind made her change her way of thinking.

Practicing yoga was one of the best things she did for herself. For the first time, she learned to breathe. She learned how to appreciate the moment. As with everything she did, Patricia went all out and attended classes four to five days a week. She had reached the point of feeling bliss in her practice. She felt euphoric and often thought that she was floating. Similar to the experience she had with her dreams, but in a more profound, loving, and relaxed way.

Patricia liked it so much that she hired the owner of the studio to give her private lessons. He was in his 40s, good-looking, with a muscular build and large stature. Patricia found him pleasant, but there was no physical attraction for her. During one of their sessions, as he helped her with a pose, his hands ended up around her waist. He pulled her in tight, pushed her on the mat, and tried to kiss her. *Not again*, she thought. Before she knew it, her auto-response was to kick him in the groin and walk off, but not without first confronting him for his behavior. He claimed to have misread her, which only infuriated Patricia. By now, she concluded that women were targets for reckless men, and many had a long way to go to learn respect. But she was not going to be a victim. Patricia was not going to let his behavior deter her from the practice, nor would she take responsibility for his actions. It made her think of Elizabeth and her situation. She decided to give it one more try and see if she could convince Elizabeth to call off the wedding.

The two sisters met for lunch. Patricia told Elizabeth about her concerns and how things may escalate in the future. "Think of your future children," Patricia pleaded. "Remember all the violence and torment we went through." But Elizabeth was convinced that this was different from their childhood; she was blind to the similarities. Patricia recognized her denial and, at that moment, knew there was nothing else she could say or do. And so the wedding was to go on. It would be the first major celebration of its kind in their family.

Some good things came from the wedding. Maria reconciled with Tony, and Uncle Juan came down for the celebration. It had been a very long time since Patricia had seen Juan. The encounter was emotional for him. From the moment he saw her, he began to cry, overcome with grief and apologetic for ever having doubted her. Patricia consoled him and assured him she had no ill will. It was ironic that she was comforting him after all that had happened.

It was a beautiful wedding. The venue was outdoors, with perfect weather. Unsure of what the future may bring for the couple, all Patricia could do was wish them well. Tears rolled down her face as she saw Elizabeth walk down the aisle. All the painful emotions Patricia felt as a child hovered over her, but this was not the day to let them overtake her. She needed to put them aside and focus on the moment. Elizabeth was happy, and her family was together.

CHAPTER 30

More Than Water Required

P atricia and Art traveled all around the world together. Her job gave them many opportunities for unique experiences, and his job afforded them the time and money to experience extravagant adventures. They worked hard and lived life, but Patricia was still not happy. She put off her wishes to have a family, hoping that Art would come around one day to want the same things she wanted. It caused her much pain. Patricia's tactic became to ignore the pain and instead make excuses to replace it by setting near-impossible goals attached to rewards. In her mind, broken aspects of her life needed fixing, which is why she could not have a family of her own. There was a list of achievements she was required to have before getting what she wanted. *You can move on if you are capable of achieving these tasks.* Patricia chose to be naïve and not see things for what they really were. Art could not commit and instead of moving forward with her wishes, she took blame and ownership of his lack of commitment.

One of her biggest fears was still water, so she took it on as a challenge. There was a university near the house with an outdoor Olympic-sized pool. She enrolled in adult swimming lessons taught by the college students. Patricia thought to herself, *What did these kids do to deserve this job?* Feeling silly for her handicap, she approached it with the attitude of erasing a part of her past that no longer served her; this gave the classes more meaning and purpose.

The lessons were easy at first. Patricia did know how to swim. After all, it was just that water made her panic. There was always a connection between water and significant events in her life. Patricia felt if she could overcome those fears, she could overcome the obstacles in her life. There were definite connections that she had been unable to decipher.

With the sessions starting in the shallow part of the pool, she was comfortable, feeling like she was flying through the lessons. Here, she felt no fear or anxiety. *This is not so bad. As a matter of fact, this is easy, just like riding a bike.* The program was two weeks long. After the second week, they would go into the deep part, the 12-foot pool. That is when the panic set in, and reality struck. Once they got to that point, she started to feel hopeless, and her enthusiasm dropped, as being in the pool was no longer easy. It had nothing to do with skill—it was about the emotional barrier she built around the water, just like the barriers she had built around her emotions. When things got tough in life, Patricia would overcome them by dissociating. While it helped her get over tough situations, she never really dealt with them. While interacting with water, she could not disassociate; Patricia had to face it head-on or drown. She wanted to quit but knew she needed to go through the process.

During the second week, she had to muster up all the courage within her to make it through the class. Unfortunately, she was no further along than when she started. Being in the deep water still made her panic. It was a mental hold that required more than swim lessons, but instead of addressing the real issue, she marked it as a failed task and punished herself by denying what she wanted. Patricia continued with the same destructive pattern she had learned as a child. It was a constant roller coaster ride of emotions. Finally, she decided to give it a break and move on to something else.

Patricia started to remember her visualization exercise. She had stopped practicing and decided it was the time to return to it, only this time, the visualization of ridding her fear of water and having a family of her own provoked tears. Having her own family was not something that would vanish from her desires. It was too important. Children were part of her destiny; she knew that. Being a good mother would not be a problem. All the hard work put into becoming a better person and arming herself with the skills necessary for the job needed to manifest themselves soon.

Patricia knew it was not all Art's fault. She had set many things aside, such as having a family and keeping friends, and she wanted to make changes. Patricia had always distanced herself from people, but it was more pronounced now, and Art made it easy for her to hide. She was waiting on Art and putting everyone else aside. She was still denying herself what she wanted. Art was comfortable in the relationship as he was getting what he needed and was in charge of making the decisions pertaining to their lives. Control was essential to Art, and it was becoming more and more apparent. Patricia did not want to lose herself any longer, and while her love for Art was deep, things did not feel right.

I need someone to talk to about this. Patricia once again debated how to approach Art on the topic of children. She mentally prepared herself for the worst, knowing what needed to happen if he did not come around. *Elizabeth may advise the best way to approach the issue.* Before she could make the call, the phone rang, and it was Elizabeth.

"So strange," said Patricia. "I was getting ready to call you."

"I have news," Elizabeth said without a pause. "I'm pregnant!" Her enthusiasm came through the phone. Elizabeth did not get an immediate response. Patricia was shocked into silence.

"Congratulations!" the words finally stumbled out of Patricia's mouth. The timing of the news could not have been worse. She knew she needed to put things on hold and wait. She could not ruin this event for her sister.

The coming of a baby was good news, but Elizabeth was still having problems in her marriage. Armando was no better than before they got married. He was belligerent and sometimes would disappear for days. Elizabeth was dismissive of the chaos surrounding their marriage and distanced herself from it. Since she did not talk about what was going on, Patricia was unsure how she handled it. One thing was for sure, Patricia needed to stand by her sister and be supportive without judgment.

From the outside looking in, Elizabeth seemed to have it all: friends, success at work, and a growing family. She had managed to survive her childhood home life by being a straight-A student and controlling her academic path. Now she was staying afloat in her adult home life by climbing the corporate ladder and having a successful career. But the facade hid a tremendous amount of pain behind those walls.

Baby Kate was born, and things were going very well until the newness of it all disappeared. Emulating a good mother, Maria spent a lot of time helping Elizabeth with the baby, which gave her a front-row seat to Elizabeth's personal life. Maria was a constant observer of the drama between Elizabeth and Armando: the fighting, screaming, and disrespect. Discretion was never one of Maria's top traits, and she did not think twice about sharing what she saw with everyone else.

Maria would call Patricia often to tell her about things that happened at Elizabeth's house. Many times, it was more than she could take, but she dared not tell Maria. Patricia listened, knowing that Maria needed to vent, realizing her mother had flashbacks to the days of Antonio. The fact that Maria never dealt with her issues made things linger, and now she was reliving her past through her youngest daughter.

Finally, the time had come for Patricia to talk to Art. She approached it the best way she could, but there was only one way to say it. Patricia had never learned to express her feelings, wants, and needs, and the words did not just roll off her tongue. She finally spoke about how she felt, expressing her desire to have a family. But Art was not capable of connecting emotionally with Patricia. Unable to finish her thoughts, Art interrupted. As the words were coming out of his mouth, Patricia froze. She knew by the look on his face that the answer would not be any different than before.

"I do not want a family." Art's words echoed in Patricia's head.

"I understand how you feel, but we don't share the same sentiment. I need to follow my heart," Patricia uttered, her face stained with tears. Her heart ached.

On the other hand, Art was pragmatic about the situation. "Do what you need to do," he said, and then walked off. He was not expressive, lacking the sensitivity or patience to discuss it with her. Instead, he simply dismissed her and the subject.

Feeling shut down and frustrated, Patricia knew she needed to move on, but she felt stuck.

She doubted herself, wondering if it was the right thing to do. Was it worth it? *I'm finally in a relationship, financially stable, and productive—but still unhappy.* The question repeated itself in her head, always coming up with the same answer. She had plans to move out, but she kept waiting for him to change his mind. That moment never came.

Patricia looked for a place to go, knowing that she feared being alone. She asked Elizabeth if she could move in temporarily. Elizabeth was always supportive and agreed. Patricia went home and packed her bags, still waiting for a reaction from Art. But he stayed true to his words and did not stop her.

Patricia threw herself into work. With a heavy travel schedule, it was easy to stay distracted. On one of her trips, she began to feel sick. She ignored it and chalked it up to exhaustion and dehydration, not thinking anything of it. When returning home, she was still not feeling well and decided to go to the doctor. After some tests, the doctor came back with a big announcement. Patricia was pregnant. She could not believe her ears. She was ecstatic, but at the same time, worried. Patricia assumed that Art would think that he got tricked into fatherhood.

While they were apart, Art had second thoughts and asked her to come back. Even though he still ignored the fact that she wanted to have a family, Patricia returned to him without giving him the news of her pregnancy. Part of her felt that it was wrong to keep it from him, but she was nervous and did not know how to handle it if he rejected her again. She thought about her reaction as a child when she found out that Maria was pregnant with Elizabeth. It was a shock at the time, but it turned out to be one of the best things that came from her parents' relationship. The thought consoled her, and she felt that Art would come around.

CHAPTER 31

Revealing Secrets

The holidays were approaching, and Patricia was about eight weeks pregnant. She still had not told anyone. Art's mom, Sue, wanted a grandchild more than anything, so Patricia decided to share the news with her under the condition that she would not say anything to Art.

Sue could not contain her excitement. Tears of joy rolled down her face as she jumped up and down. She promised not to tell anyone, but encouraged Patricia to tell Art sooner rather than later. Patricia told Art's sister next and eventually told Maria and Elizabeth. Everyone was very supportive, but they all showed concerns about her lack of transparency with Art.

About four months into her pregnancy, she was starting to show and had no choice but to tell Art about the baby. She planned out the day and time to tell him. She made reservations at one of their favorite restaurants. It was a loud venue with lots of people, so she knew he would not be able to overreact. They went out, as usual, and Art was completely unsuspecting, just like all the other times they had gone out to eat.

They arrived at the restaurant to find that celebrity chef, Jacques Pépin, was there to celebrate a new cookbook. The restaurant owner, with whom they had become friends, invited the couple to sit at his table. Patricia so badly wanted to say no, but before she could say anything, Art accepted. Unfortunately, she could not tell him with their new tablemates, so it would have to wait. It turned out to be an incredible night, an experience that would have been magical under any other circumstance.

She tried to tell him the next day when they were home, but he was on several work calls until late. Finally, when he was in his office and off the phone, she walked in and blurted out the news. "I'm pregnant!" Art looked up at Patricia and asked, "What did you say?" He could not believe what he was hearing. "We discussed having a family, and I told you how I felt." He went on to reiterate his remarks. "I also told you how I felt, and this is important to me. I don't think you even know what you want." Patricia felt Art needed someone to guide him emotionally, and it was her duty to change him.

As expected, he did not take the news very well. Once he was over the shock, he asked how long she had known. Unable to lie, she told him the truth, that the pregnancy was four months along. He was angry, feeling trapped, and now betrayed that she did not tell him sooner.

She could not bear the disappointment. She left for Maria's house to vent. On the way there, she called Art's mom. "He is mad at me. I told him about the pregnancy, and he is upset, feels like I betrayed him." Sue tried to console her. "He will come around. Don't upset yourself. I will talk to him."

She arrived at Maria's, who advised her to give him time to come around. After a couple of hours, Patricia drove back home, unsure of what to expect. When she arrived, Art hugged her and held her close. He approached her with calmness and understanding. Sue had called her son with some words of wisdom and advice.

Patricia's doctor's appointment was the following week, and she was due for an ultrasound. She asked Art to accompany her. Art was still in shock, but agreed. Patricia felt it would help him get involved by seeing the little life inside of her developing. Sure enough, when Art saw the baby, he could not help but smile. His face softened and his eyes filled up with tears. "It's a girl!" revealed the doctor.

"I'm going to be a father. We should start thinking of names!" shouted Art.

Patricia was excited, feeling free to get the house and nursery ready. Art was supportive but hands-off in the coming months, with life going on as usual. Finally, after much work, the nursery was assembled and the doors were closed until the baby's arrival.

When she was seven months along, Patricia was in Amsterdam for a conference. Art joined her, as he often did in those days. It was a work-babymoon trip. They enjoyed dining out and sightseeing in the beautiful city. Unfamiliar with the lifestyle in Amsterdam, they walked into a café, simply thinking that it was a coffee house. Patricia, obviously now showing, sat down at the table while Art went to order. Unfortunately, coffee was not the only highlight of the menu. It was a cannabis café. They laughed at themselves and left right away.

Visiting the Van Gogh Museum was at the top of the to-do list while in Amsterdam. Van Gogh was one of her favorite artists, and this museum housed the most extensive collection of his masterpieces. The arts center was across town from the hotel, and they planned to take the underground there. Unfortunately, while going down the stairs, Patricia slipped and fell. Art rushed to her side and helped her up. She was fine, but startled. Art escorted her back to the hotel to rest. A couple of hours later, Patricia felt better, and they made their way to the museum, which lived up to its reputation. Patricia and Art flowed from one painting to the other, looking at each one in detail. They discussed the paintings and enjoyed the day, ending with dinner at a local café. It was a beautiful night, and they walked back to the hotel, passing several coffee houses and laughing as they recalled their earlier mishap.

On the flight home, she decided this would be her last trip until after the baby was born. She was not going to take any risks with the remaining months of her pregnancy.

A couple of months went by, and Patricia's due date was approaching. Art's mother could not wait for the birth of her first grandchild. Her excitement was more than anyone could bear, and she came to stay with them three days before the due date. Sue was bothered that they were having a baby out of wedlock. Art had proposed to Patricia months earlier, but Patricia was upset that he had not done it sooner, and she refused. She felt he was proposing out of obligation, and she did not want that. Art's mom was not having it. So, along with Maria, they marched the couple down to the justice of the peace, and they got married. *Shotgun wedding*. That is what Patricia thought about the whole thing. None of it mattered to her anymore. She was going to love her baby more than anything in the world, and Art, too, would love the baby. He just needed time to realize that children were part of his destiny as well.

Finally, the due date had arrived. It was a Monday. Sue was the most impatient, insisting Patricia get checked.

"It is time," Sue kept repeating. Sue insisted that Patricia go to the doctor for a check-up. She drove Patricia to the doctor and while in the middle of her appointment, Patricia's water broke. They rushed her next door to the hospital. Now it really *was* time.

Patricia did not want medication, insisting on having a natural delivery. Halfway through and no longer able to tolerate the pain, she called out for any kind of painkillers they could give her. She would take anything.

"Too late," the doctor commented. Patricia insisted again, even begged. Finally, the doctor managed to give her something. Maria,

Sue, Art, and Elizabeth were in the delivery room. The painkillers finally knocked her out, and she was unable to push. Art woke her, and 18 hours later, Elise arrived!

Elise was beautiful. She could have been a Gerber baby with her cherub face. She was angelic, with creamy, white skin and yellow rays of hair. Patricia insisted that it could not be her baby; Elise looked nothing like her. But she most certainly was, and she felt an instant bond with Elise.

Sue stayed on for a few days. She was a joy to have around, making everyone laugh and helping make serious, complicated tasks doable. Unfortunately, her stay was short. Art's dad was away, working on a cargo ship much of the time and only coming home every two months. Sue needed to get back to her house and take care of things there. Patricia was sad to see her leave.

Art fell in love with Elise from the moment he saw her. Patricia was not surprised; she always knew he would love her. However, his work pace did not slow down, and his travel continued. Patricia continued to work as well. Even though she had maternity leave, calls were still coming in, and she was required to attend meetings. Things became overwhelming trying to juggle it all, but she was persistent and stubborn. The need to prove that she could do it all was a big driving force. But it was all worth it because Patricia felt love, true love, for the first time in her life. Now, knowing what it meant to have unconditional love, she felt complete.

Elise was a good baby, slept most of the night, and was a good eater. Maria would come around to visit, but she spent most of her time with Elizabeth. Patricia never demanded much of Maria's time. She was independent and knew there were always consequences to asking for Maria's help. Patricia's relationship with Elizabeth got stronger, with their baby girls only one year apart. The two sisters had plans to spend holidays together so their children could grow up with one another. They envisioned them playing, dressing alike, and taking pictures together. Patricia wanted to create happy and healthy memories for Elise, unlike the memories she had of her own childhood.

Patricia was excited to celebrate the holidays that year. She cooked a big dinner, invited their family and friends over for a festive celebration, and did things she'd never done before, like buy a Christmas tree and ornaments. Along with the tree, Patricia decorated the house and ordered personalized ornaments for everyone, including their family pet, Chili. It was a pivotal point in her life, and for the first time, she felt happy during the holidays. Finally, she could rewrite bad memories with good ones. Everyone was together. Art's parents visited, and so did Patricia's. Baby Elise was tiny but powerful, able to bring everyone together into one place.

After the holidays passed, they got a call from Art's mom, who needed to talk to them. She asked that they, along with her daughter, Anne, drive out to the house in Austin. The urgency resonated in her voice. So they obliged and left the next day. Anne arrived from college, and Patricia and Art met her at the house.

The mood was gloomy, and the place was dark, with all the lights turned off. Anne sat alone in the living room, and Art's mother was sleeping in her bedroom. Anne greeted them warmly, happy to see them, but also ready for what seemed like foreboding news.

They went into Sue's bedroom and woke her. She looked different, tired, her face lifeless. Patricia immediately knew something was wrong. Art's mother was always smiling and laughing, even during the most challenging times. The three stood by the bed, dreading the words that may come out of her mouth. Slowly, she sat up in bed, pale, her eyes half shut, and with much hesitation, announced she had been diagnosed with cancer.

Devastated, Patricia could not hold back her tears. She felt such a strong love for Sue that the news broke her heart. Art was sad, but he was immediately thinking of how to fix the problem; this was a big difference between Art and Patricia. Patricia was emotional and wore her heart on her sleeve, while Art was pragmatic and did not like to dwell on things.

Sue had been ill long before being diagnosed, but had refused to go to the doctor. She finally went on a fluke, thinking she had pneumonia. X-rays detected a mass that triggered additional tests that eventually revealed aggressive cancer. At this point, it was too late to take any life-changing actions. The doctor had told her she had six months to live.

Patricia's thoughts filled with grief; Elise would not have the privilege of growing up with her grandmother Sue and getting to know what an amazing woman she was. At first, it angered Patricia. She could not understand why Art's mom hadn't taken better care of herself and why she did not value her life as much as everyone else's. But the anger did not last long. She knew that at that point, all she could do was love Sue while she was still with them and that this was Sue's journey to take.

Sue's cancer was aggressive, and she was very ill very quickly. She was undergoing chemotherapy and radiation, which caused her hair to fall out. Unfortunately, the treatments didn't seem to work, and Sue was frustrated. Doctors assumed it was pancreatic cancer but never confirmed for sure, as the cancer had spread too quickly.

Meanwhile, true to her character, Sue wanted to go shopping for wigs and asked Patricia to join her. They went to many shops and tried all types of wigs, colored ones, long ones, short ones. They laughed so hard, they forgot the reason they were purchasing the wigs in the first place. Throughout the process, Sue found a reason to smile and make everyone feel that things would be okay. She did not want to talk about her cancer—she wanted to spend as much time as possible with Elise and for life to proceed as usual.

But time had other plans, as the cancer progressed quickly, and she was no longer able to drive back and forth from Houston to Austin, forcing Sue to stay full-time in their Austin home, with Anne regularly coming to check on her. The medications were not working, and Sue began trying alternative treatments like juicing and experimental methods, but the cancer was taking over her body. Despite her ability to stay positive, she was weakening and could no longer hold food down.

Art decided that it would be better for everyone if Sue stayed with them in Houston. Patricia was home all day with Elise and could keep an eye on her. Art drove to Austin to pick his mother up and drive her back to Houston. She was only there a short time before things started to worsen. She was not eating, and this frustrated Art. He tried to force her to take energy shakes, but Sue just batted them away. Finally, one morning, in total aggravation, Art yelled at her to take the drink. But with all the strength she had, Sue raised from the bed and asked him to leave, so he did. It was the last morning she was at their house.

Art desperately wanted Sue to get better but, unfortunately, did not have the competence to relay his sentiments to his sick mother.

Feeling like she was at the end of her time, Sue asked Patricia to get her a prescription. Only this was no ordinary prescription. Patricia left Elise with a sitter and followed the directions unequivocally. She knew this was important for Sue, and she didn't want to let her down or make a mistake.

The first stop was at the medical center, to a clinic located in their basement. There, Patricia handed them the paper Sue had given her, trading it in for a prescription. The next step was to go to the pharmacy and fill the prescription. It all seemed very mysterious, so Patricia asked the pharmacist what the pills were.

"You should ask the patient requesting them," the pharmacist bluntly said. Patricia rushed home with the medicine and asked Sue.

"It is time," Sue calmly replied. "Please bring me water." Patricia ran upstairs to get the water. When she returned, Sue laid her head down on the pillow. Patricia noticed Sue already had water and sent her out of the room to take the medication in private. Patricia sat by her bedside in case she needed anything, but in reality, she was scared to leave

Sue alone. Patricia did not want to lose her. Sue was calm, no longer in pain, sleeping peacefully. Patricia went up to check on Elise. When she returned, Sue's breath was shallow, and she was unresponsive.

Patricia did not know what to do other than call 911. An ambulance rushed Sue to the hospital, where doctors asked Patricia to reach out to all of Sue's loved ones and tell them to come as soon as possible. Patricia was emotional but somehow kept it together long enough to call Art at work, Anne at school, and Art's dad overseas.

Now with everyone at the hospital, the doctors informed the family there was nothing else they could do. Sue was moved to hospice. Patricia took Elise to the hospice to see Sue. Sue recognized the baby, and instantly, she lovingly smiled at her and took Elise into her arms as she pressed her tightly onto her chest. Elise was eight months old, and it would be the last time she would feel the warmth of her precious grandmother. But it would not be the last time she would feel her presence or hear her voice. Anne and her dad sat by Sue's side until her passing.

Although Patricia felt as if she had lost her own mother, her bond with Sue had been one she had never expected to have, and she was grateful for knowing her. Patricia tried to reach out to Art with her feelings, but he was reluctant to talk. Before Sue's death, Art was in denial, and now with her gone, he remained in that space; he never really accepted the loss of his mother. Sue was the only person Art felt comfortable talking to, and he loved her dearly. To lose her was devastating, but he was not ready to face the fact that she was gone.

Nevertheless, Patricia would make sure that Elise remembered her grandmother. She told her daughter stories and showed her pictures. She wanted to make sure her spirit lived on in their house and within their family's heart.

Throughout the years, they felt Sue's presence. For example, one day, Art and Patricia were arguing in the kitchen. Elise, two years old, suddenly yelled at them.

"Stop arguing. Grandma said so!" They immediately stopped and looked around. They wondered if they had heard correctly. Other incidents made it evident that Elise was somehow spiritually connected to her Grandma Sue. Patricia also felt her presence whenever she was in need. Her voice would resonate to soothe and enlighten, helping her through tough times. Sue kept giving even after her passing.

Soon Patricia had to go back to work, so they needed to hire a nanny. As luck would have it, the mother of someone Patricia worked with was available. Anna was a warm, loving woman that had three grown children of her own. She had just left her job and was looking for a part-time position working with children. Among her many traits, Spanish was her primary language. Patricia was happy about this, hoping that Elise would pick up the language and become fluent. She had tried to speak to Elise in Spanish, but now, two people engaging with her in Spanish would be even better.

Anna made Patricia feel comfortable, treating Elise as if she were one of her own. Traveling a lot for work, she needed someone who could take care of the baby as she would. Patricia always felt guilty about having to miss holidays and events due to work engagements. Even though she was doing everything to the best of her abilities, she was full of guilt, never proud of herself or relishing the moments or appreciating the quality time she did spend with Elise. It was her way of operating, causing her to resent her job and wonder if it was all worth it. Patricia's primary focus had been trying to build a career for a better life of success. Now that this child had entered her life and swept her off her feet, was it wrong to want to make Elise the main focus?

Subconsciously, there was also another reason she was not giving up her job. Patricia always had one foot in the door and one out, never trusting anyone. She needed to be strong and resilient, always prepared for battle. Even though she was in a stable relationship with Art, in the back of her mind, she did not let her guard down. Financial security was also vital to her existence; not wanting to stay in a relationship because of economic dependency.

Elise was a game-changer in more ways than one for Patricia. One of the most significant gifts she brought with her was awarding her mother the ability to make friends with other moms and create bonds she had never had before. Elise was a true light for Patricia, helping her heal from her past. Elise turned out to be everything Patricia wanted to be. Elise was social and talented at everything she did—dance, gymnastics, music. She inspired Patricia to live outside her comfort zone. It was hard to believe a child could have so much influence.

Patricia made several attempts to bond with Art and improve the family dynamics. However, he was still closed off, throwing himself into work and becoming even more hands-off with family matters. Since the birth of Elise, Patricia did not pay the same attention to him. Patricia assumed he felt jealous, and in reality, since Elise's birth, Patricia didn't need him the same way, and he must have sensed it. It was not something that happened overnight. Art's lack of ability to fully commit and engage wore Patricia down and she managed to find true love from another source. It was a complicated situation. Yet, Patricia tried not to dwell on it too much.

CHAPTER 32

Never Give Up

All the pieces were in place for a happy life, but as Elise got older, Patricia craved a second child. Surprisingly, so did Art. Patricia started seeing how Elise was becoming more and more independent, and while independence is what she wanted for Elise, she missed having a baby in the house. So Patricia started doing everything she could to get pregnant. She became a vegetarian and stopped drinking alcohol and coffee. She even started consuming wheatgrass.

Months went by, and nothing was happening. When all her efforts failed, she changed directions and refused to give in to failure. The second child became a focal point for her and a challenge. She submerged herself in yoga, started acupuncture, and researched all the natural ways to get pregnant.

Two years went by, and they were still not successful; she was 42 years old, and the challenge was real. Patricia never thought she'd find herself in this situation, unsure if it was a fertility problem or a mental block. So she started taking things to another level, measuring hormone levels and days of ovulation. Stubborn and willful, she was set on getting pregnant on her own accord and became obsessed with becoming an expert on the subject while sticking to her plan of not going to a fertility clinic nor involving doctors in the process.

Patricia's actions went so far as to find an online lab that would send her orders for a monthly hormone test to measure if her efforts were working. For mental stimulation, she signed up for several inspirational blogs that talked about success stories on infertility, read articles about impossible dreams becoming possible, and took herbal teas from the acupuncturist that would leave her nauseous for days. It went on until she exhausted all her options, and her will started to dwindle.

Art was talking less and less about a second child and accepted that there might not be one. Deep down, this infuriated Patricia, as she secretly blamed him for taking so long to have the first child. Unable to understand how he was not taking drastic actions like she was, she questioned how he could be so complacent with this when he was usually so obsessed with everything else. But blaming Art did not resolve the problem and left Patricia with a desire she could not fulfill.

Meanwhile, Elizabeth had her second child, a boy. While Patricia was happy for her, reality sank in, and depression took over. Sadness consumed her, having no enthusiasm for anything. One morning, while getting her wheatgrass, she overheard someone talking about suicide, and she felt even worse. She could relate to the subject matter. Suicidal feelings had always been with her. Buried deep down inside, she could feel them calling to her on occasion. She would never mention it or talk to anyone about it because it was embarrassing and didn't even make sense to her. Now that she had a family, it seemed impossible that the thoughts could still be there. She recalled the woman from the hospital that was suicidal with children and how she had judged her, and now she was in the same situation.

Finally, she decided to give up on her mission to get pregnant again. She thought of two significant failures: first, the fear of water, and now, the non-existent pregnancy. But she knew repeated failures to achieve having another child would deepen her sorrow, and Patricia feared going back to her old ways. It was best not to wallow in sorrow, so she focused on taking care of Elise and shifting her energy back to work.

Distraction at work was easy. Her marketing firm had taken on a big client during this time. Patricia had become close to the client. They were a group of young entrepreneurs from Latin America that pulled all their money together and disrupted the traditional hotel model. It was an interesting project for Patricia. She liked disruption and breaking traditional molds. The property was in the jungle, with private pools and unheard-of rates, creating even more significant demand. The concept and the marketing were all aligned at the right time, making it fun and innovative.

The commitment to this project required international travel. It was a crossroads for Patricia; she needed to invest more time in order to further her career, but that would mean spending less time with her family. It was the opposite of what she was trying to achieve just months earlier. Patricia was conflicted.

Her guilt kicked in, and Patricia decided she would discuss how she was feeling with Art. Their relationship was unique in that they did not consult with each other on major decisions. Instead, Art worked and provided for the family. What spare time he had was allocated to eating out or vacationing. Patricia had learned to live in this environment, as she did not like to be controlled and rather appreciated the freedom. Patricia worked and contributed to the family finances, but it was always well marked that Art was the main provider. It was important for him that everyone, especially Patricia, recognize his efforts.

Patricia planned a date night, she secured a sitter, and they went out. During the evening, Patricia told Art how she felt. "I'm sad about not being able to have another child. It makes me feel like a failure, and

I'm afraid I will not be able to overcome it and become depressed. There is a new project at work, offering a challenge with an opportunity for growth and a good distraction. But I feel guilty."

Art had a perplexed look on his face. "Are you saying it is my fault we did not have a second child?" Patricia just stared at him in disbelief. "Did you not hear what I said? Why does everything have to be about you?" Patricia said. The conversation brought her back to Elizabeth's graduation, where Maria asked if Patricia's breakdown was based on something *she* had done. Neither Art nor Maria were capable of connecting with her and offering true empathy. Patricia felt alone after their conversation. It was becoming more and more apparent to her that she had little support.

Patricia made the decision to invest the time into work but realized that she was going to need help to accomplish everything she had set out to do. She decided to hire a nanny for Elise. Only Elise was now seven years old and reluctant to have someone besides Patricia taking her to where she needed to be. Patricia offered a different approach and invited Elise to interview the nannies and pick the one she liked best. It would be a fun project, and that way, Elise would feel she had a choice.

Patricia began choosing a few candidates for Elise. They had narrowed it down to two. Elise got to pick the meeting point for the interviews. She decided on the local ice cream shop they frequented. The first candidate to arrive was a recent UT graduate dressed professionally and carrying a portfolio with her resume. Elise had a series of questions she asked. The young girl played along and answered all of Elise's questions, which consisted of things like, "Would you allow me to stay up late?" After Elise finished, Patricia asked her own set of questions.

The second candidate arrived, and she could not be more opposite of the first. She had a series of Frida Kahlo tattoos on her, body piercings, and was dressed in jeans and a t-shirt. Again, they followed the same protocol with the questions, only Elise went so far as to ask about the tattoos, and the young girl kindly explained to Elise what they were.

As promised, Elise picked the candidate she liked most and chose Lindy, the young girl with the tattoos. It turned out to be the best decision they had ever made. Lindy was kind and respectful, going above and beyond, and managed to become friends with Elise. In addition, Lindy was a creative and talented artist, inspiring Elise to make music and draw.

Elise was happy, but missed her mother. Some of Patricia's trips would take her away on special occasions. One year, she missed Mother's Day, then, she missed Halloween, one of Elise's favorite times of the year. It was bittersweet to get the picture of Elise and Lindy carving a pumpkin. The picture also served as a reminder of the moments she was missing. Patricia knew that soon, Elise would be too big for those activities. Nonetheless, Patricia stuck to her decision.

CHAPTER 33

Persistence Pays Off

Having established a strong working foundation with the investors of the Mexican hotel, they invited Patricia and Art to invest in a project they were working on in Argentina. The project consisted of a vineyard with private homes and a hotel. But first, they needed to promote the wine, to raise the interest for the rest of the master plan. Art loved wine and wanted in. Neither Patricia nor Art knew anything about the business, but they jumped in head-first. It was a significant development that would take up even more time from the family. Nevertheless, Art was insistent, and Patricia saw it as the next step on her journey. She had worked hard for recognition, building strong connections with influential people, and now she was in a position she never imagined herself contemplating.

And so it was Art and Patricia who took on the new task of import-ing wine and marketing the brand. At first, Art became involved by taking charge of the logistics. But later, like many things he was involved in, he lost interest, and it all fell on Patricia, leaving her with a workload like never before. She was doing two jobs, her marketing job and her wine job, *and* being a mother. Thank goodness for Lindy, or else Patricia would have reached her breaking point. Stress and despair were already starting to creep in, and Patricia started to realize she could no longer hide behind thousands of projects.

Patricia began to exercise obsessively, and her eating disorder returned. She was going days without eating. Elise would come up and ask her a question, and Patricia's answers were short and sharp. Oftentimes, she would catch a glimpse of herself in the mirror, and she looked angry, to the point that she often had to do a double-take. Is this what she had become? A miserable person who lashed out at her family?

Elise had just gotten a phone and was recording everything in sight. She sat in the kitchen while Patricia stood in the kitchen eating a snack. As Patricia was eating, Elise proceeded to ask her a series of questions and recorded her. Unaware of the recording, Patricia answered with one word and never looked up to make eye contact with Elise. Later, Elise showed her mom the video. Patricia was startled. She saw her mother in herself. She had become what she feared most, an angry and unattached Maria. It broke her heart.

Unable to understand what was happening, Patricia tried to make sense of it all in her head. Yes, she had tried to get pregnant without success, but so did thousands of other women. Why did she have to take it so personally and struggle with feelings of inadequacy, shame, and failure? Was it all in her mind? Was it a punishment for her past? Even though she was not responsible, somehow, she managed to make it her responsibility. Even worse, she was lashing out at the people she loved most.

Having a family of her own had not been a trivial desire. It was a way to make good on her past, but again, Patricia refused to speak about how she felt. Instead, she put on a front that everything was great, and now she was faced with struggles and sadness. Art continued traveling and was engulfed in his work. Nothing was ever enough, and every-thing was measured by monetary growth. They bought a bigger house every five years, made large purchases, and traveled the world, but they failed to create a bond, not only for the two of them, but also for their family. Patricia was just as guilty; she liked living in a nice house and having success. She thought the material things made her powerful. Instead, she felt defeated.

Her life was beginning to unravel. All the feelings she had pushed down were creeping up and finally rearing their ugly heads. Patricia needed to face her demons. They were sitting there, waiting for her to deal with them. They had a mind of their own and could no longer wait. The fear that hovered over her as a child and the continuous blaming was back. Patricia's anxiety was growing stronger, with no desire to con-tinue working. All she wanted to do was sit in bed and watch television. As the days went by, Patricia stopped going into the office and stopped talking to everyone she knew.

Elise came home from school with Lindy and found her mom lying on the couch. Elise walked over. "Why are you not at work? You're never home this much." Patricia sat up as she lovingly looked at Elise and recalled when she would sit outside Maria's bedroom door, waiting for her to get up. She remembered the loneliness that came over her, wanting her mother to engage. "Mommy is hiding," Patricia replied with tears rolling down her face.

Elise grabbed Patricia's hand. "Mommy, I love you, and I see you, so you're not hiding. It's not working." At that moment, she realized Elise was right, and she could not hide. There were too many people depend-ing on her, so leaving things undone was not an option.

Patricia mustered up the courage to go back into the office. She sought out a therapist and made a plan to relinquish some of her responsibilities in order to spend more time with Elise.

The arguing with Art increased as Patricia harbored ill will towards him. She was in a different setting than when she was a little girl, but even though Patricia was no longer being told she could not achieve anything, she was surrounded by people who never gave her credit or appreciation. Patricia was an adult who had succeeded in many aspects of her life, but still felt empty. Art was not one to ever give praise or encouragement, nor did he recognize the work that she had done. Sam also disregarded her.

Patricia recalled the success that her clients from Mexico achieved based on the action plans that were implemented under her direction. The success came from working as a team, but Sam took all the credit. Patricia recognized that she was still surrounded by people who made her feel invisible.

Patricia would close this chapter in her life and finish what she started. Partially for self-satisfaction, but deep down inside, Patricia knew she was also seeking approval. Desperate for someone to say, "You did it, you succeeded, I'm proud of you." What she did not realize at the time was that the approval she so craved was actually from her parents. It was a void that would go empty for years, until realizing she had the power to be proud and believe in *herself*, and that would have to be enough, because her parents would never be able to give her what she longed for from them.

Leaving all the negative feelings behind, Patricia thought of Elise and reminded herself she had a daughter who looked up to her. She wanted Elise to grow up to be strong and positive, and it was her job to show her how to be a strong woman.

She had things to do and refused to give in to the self-talk and doubt. People depended on her. So, sticking to her character, she shifted directions, and instead of breaking down, Patricia marched forward, hoping that someone would be there to notice when it was all said and done. She dug deep and put her best foot forward.

Her creative side surfaced, and she put together a plan that would bring the wine business success. Patricia and Art were getting featured in newspapers and magazines, creating a demand from consumers.

Finally, things were starting to take shape, and the stress began to subside. She began to feel relief and made space to breathe and relax and enjoy the success.

Meanwhile, Lindy was holding down the fort at home with Elise and Chili. Lindy loved dogs and treated him like royalty. However, they noticed he was not himself. Chili was no longer showing the same enthusiasm and was refusing to eat, which was rare, as eating was the highlight of his day. As time went on, he became weaker and weaker. Patricia didn't think much of it until Lindy brought it to her attention.

Patricia took Chili to the vet. After tests and some blood work, the vet came out and informed Patricia that he could feel some lumps on Chili's neck. Further blood work revealed an illness. He could not confirm for sure, but he thought it could be cancer. She was devastated. Chili meant the world to her.

She sat down with Lindy to give her the bad news. Naturally, Lindy was upset, after all, she spent a lot of time with Chili and Elise. Lindy held back her tears. Patricia hugged Lindy and thanked her for the time and nourishment she gave to them. "You have become family," Patricia reiterated to her. Patricia realized at that moment that maybe she had been negligent in acknowledging Lindy as more than just help.

The next day, Patricia had a big day ahead of her; she had planned a big press event for the wine. The attendees were magazines and newspaper writers she had invited. The venue was to unveil a new vintage of wine. The dinner was a success but ran very late. She hurried home in hopes of seeing Elise before she went to bed. As she trudged up the stairs, she could hear her daughter's laughter coming from her bedroom. The sound started to become faint, and Patricia began to feel dizzy. Suddenly, she collapsed on the stairs.

Lindy and Elise ran to see what the noise was about. They found Patricia passed out on the landing. Lindy ran to get water as Elise sat by her mother's side. She was only out for a few seconds. As Patricia woke up, Lindy helped her and took her to lay down. She felt dizzy and clammy. "I'm fine, don't worry," she said to Lindy. "You can go home." Lindy was worried, but Patricia insisted. "Please put Elise to bed," she said as Lindy walked out.

Art was out of town, so Patricia called him to tell him what had happened. She blamed it on exhaustion, dehydration and stress over Chili. Patricia felt the need to justify what had happened even though Art's only response was, "Take it easy. I'll be home tomorrow."

The next morning, she was still feeling uneasy about having passed out the night before. *Should I take a pregnancy test?* Even though she had put pregnancy out of her head, something told her to take the test. She had a stockpile of them from when she had been trying to conceive. *Why not?* Patricia took the test and waited for a few minutes. Gradually, she picked it up and saw two lines representing positive. *No way!* She thought to herself. Patricia could not believe her eyes. So she took another one and then another. She took five in total and all five were positive.

All the times she had tried so hard to get pregnant, and now, without even trying, the tests were saying she was positive—five times over. Her entire body tingled with happiness while, at the same time, her mind began to imagine all the possible scenarios that could go wrong or that could trigger a false positive. Not wanting to get ahead of herself or give false hope, Patricia decided not to say anything until she could confirm the results. So, she scheduled a doctor's appointment for the following afternoon.

On the way to the doctor's office, Patricia began to wonder how this could have happened. Her mind went to Chili. Maybe she had manifested trading her dog's life for a child's life. *Could this be the case,* she wondered? These were the kinds of thoughts that would pop into her head. It couldn't just be a coincidence.

When Patricia arrived at the doctor's office, she found out the nurse practitioner would examine her, as the doctor was out of town. Patricia was nervous; the nurse ran all the necessary tests and confirmed she was pregnant and needed to return for an ultrasound a couple of weeks later. It was hard to contain the excitement, but she still wanted to wait before saying anything. *What if I'm overconfident and something goes wrong?*

As luck would have it, her Uncle Juan announced that he would be visiting Houston that same week. It had been a while since she had last seen him. An artist now, his paintings were terrific, and he was trying to promote them through galleries. His goal was to visit as many as possible in Houston, and knowing that Patricia was in marketing, he asked her for help with setting up appointments.

Patricia was not familiar with the world of art galleries, but Art was, so he agreed to help however he could. They decided that a preview party was in order just one week later, featuring one of the paintings Patricia had purchased from Uncle Juan. Influenced by his past demons and political stance, the painting took up about a quarter of the wall. The work was very detailed, with hidden meanings. On its own, it was a great piece, but when he explained the details, it became a masterpiece.

Juan was a complex individual. His upbringing was far from conventional. He had abandonment issues stemming from physical and mental abuse. Once, he was a successful graphic designer with social status in El Salvador. Now, due to political circumstances, he had become a refugee living in Canada, struggling to adapt and feeling like an outsider. His art reflected all those sides of him and gave him the freedom to express himself.

Patricia's ultrasound was scheduled for the day before the preview party. She went in with great excitement about being a mother again. She lay on the bed as the nurse prepared her. The ultrasound began, and Patricia's eyes remained glued to the monitor. She could not see anything. She looked back at the nurse, and her expression was not comforting. "Is everything okay?" asked Patricia. "It is a false pregnancy," the nurse announced. "It's common with people your age," she said matter of factly. "Take this pill and come back on Monday for scrapping." Patricia was in disbelief at what she was hearing. The room was cold but became colder. She slowly got off the table and dressed in a daze. They were so easy to dismiss her. She was shattered and walked away angry and upset. *How could they be so cold?* Patricia refused to take the pill and went home instead.

Not wanting to ruin the party, she proceeded to prepare for the preview show. She tried desperately to put the day's events out of her mind. Just two days ago, she was satisfied not having a second child, then she was surprised with a positive test, and now she was devastated as she was ripped from the notion of being pregnant.

During the event, Patricia walked around like a zombie. She held back tears as she smiled and made small talk. People's lips were moving, but Patricia could not hear what they were saying. She knew this feeling; it was the same way she felt when she was in school. Everything was happening around her, but she was not part of it. The event went off without a hitch, and people enjoyed Juan's interpretation of the art. Juan thanked Patricia and hugged her. He asked if all was okay as he could feel something was wrong. Patricia just shrugged and began to cry. Here they were once again, with Patricia crying and Juan unclear about what was happening. He could only think of that day in the car as he was driving her to the airport. He apologized with tears in his eyes for hurting her and hoped that whatever was going on would get better. He soon left for the airport back to Canada.

With all the distractions now gone, she could no longer take the pain and finally broke her silence. Patricia told Art, and as she did, her body collapsed into his. She could not control the tears. She told him everything, the stresses of work and trying to get pregnant. Art tried to console her and tell her that everything would be fine. He offered to take her on a weekend getaway to forget about what was happening. But Patricia chose not to go. She felt this was a punishment for the past, the present, and future happiness that she might claim—the next two days of waiting were the longest days of her life.

On the Monday morning of her doctor's appointment, an immense force took over her. Patricia fell to the ground, sobbing and asking the world, the universe, for help. She recalled this same pleading as a child. Calling out to anyone who would listen, asking for help, strength, but most of all, for her baby to be there. As her sobs subsided, she felt peace and stood up. Feeling strong and positive, she decided that she would not just go back to the doctor's office. Instead, she asked to go to the hospital and get an ultrasound done there.

"If you insist," said the nurse.

She did insist.

There was the fetus. "It was just hiding," said the technician.

And that was the beginning of her love story with her second child that lit up her world. Even before the child was born, they taught her to never give up and to never lose hope. Patricia was 44 years old and loved being pregnant. She had always felt her best during her pregnancies. Before the baby arrived, Art and Patricia had a conversation with Elise about being a big sister. Patricia wanted Elise to be happy and embrace her sibling. They would be eight years apart, just like her and Elizabeth. *Funny how history repeats itself.* She wanted to create a safe haven for her children. The best part was that her sister's children would be close to hers—something she never had as a child.

Everything she had done up to this point was all through trial and error. There were no lessons to go back and take from her childhood, only examples of what not to do. It gave her a sense of pride. She did not want to let her children down. She needed to be healthy and strong for their sake.

CHAPTER 34

Losing a Best Friend

Patricia was happy that her family was growing and embraced the moment, but she couldn't stop thinking about Chili. He was doing fine for now, but she knew the days were limited. She continued to make his food, and Chili looked forward to eating, which was a good sign. However, as the days went by, he was growing weaker and weaker, sleeping most of the time.

Lindy called while Patricia was at work one afternoon to say that Chili was in a bad state and unable to hold any food down. Patricia rushed home to tend to him, but when she arrived, it was too late. He had passed away. Luckily, Elise thought Chili was asleep. It took Patricia everything she had not to break down in front of her. Instead, she finished dinner with Elise and put her to bed.

Heartbroken, Patricia walked downstairs and fell to the ground sobbing over him. Chili was her first child, and she would never forget him.

She had planned to take him to the vet the next morning. Unfortunately, Art was out of town on business, and she knew she would need to handle all the arrangements on her own. It was a repetitive occurrence in their family, and each event left a deeper scar.

When Elise woke, Patricia helped her get ready for school and talked to her about saying her goodbyes to Chili. Elise said her farewells but did not realize it was forever. Her innocence was bliss.

Patricia called her mother and sister to tell them of Chili's passing. They offered to drive her and Chili to the vet, but Patricia refused. She needed to do that herself. She arrived at the vet and watched as they took his body away. The vet explained the cremation process. It was all very technical. "You can collect Chili's remains in two weeks," the front desk told her. It was as if she was dropping off dry cleaning and being asked to pick it up later.

A couple of months later, the family had planned a ski trip to Colorado for the holidays. It was a first, where Elizabeth and her family, Maria, and Art's sister, Anne, would all be joining. Patricia was having a hard time getting over the loss of Chili and continuously cried. Being pregnant was not helping either. Her hormones were all over the place. She considered canceling the trip but did not want to upset anyone and ruin their blended family vacation.

They left just before winter break started and would return to celebrate Christmas Eve at Elizabeth's home. The kids were excited and loved to play in the snow. Patricia tried to focus on the positives and remembered that it was Maria's first time in a winter wonderland. She wanted her mom to enjoy the beauty and have fun, so she tried to stay festive.

As the trip progressed, Patricia began to feel tension. Maria and Elizabeth seemed to be upset, and Patricia assumed they were arguing about something amongst themselves. After a while, she felt it was directed more toward her, but she was distracted by trying to deal with Chili's loss and taking care of herself. As the trip ended, the tension was thick, and neither Maria nor Elizabeth were speaking to Patricia. There was always drama during the holidays, and Patricia had no desire to bring anything up and create more tension. The trip ended, and there was no mention of any hurt feelings from either party.

As planned, Patricia, Art, and Elise went to Elizabeth's house for Christmas Eve. Armando's family was also there, and Armando had cooked a feast. The atmosphere was festive until Patricia walked into the room. Immediately seeing her, Maria and Elizabeth left the kitchen and disappeared. Patricia decided to pay no mind as her goal was to avoid all confrontation.

At one point, Elise ran to the room where her cousins were playing. Patricia followed and found Maria and Elizabeth in deep conversation. As soon as she walked into the room, they became silent. No longer able to contain herself, Patricia asked what was happening since they acted as if she had done something to upset them. Maria was the first to speak up. She complained about Patricia's dismissive behavior during the ski trip. She continued to say that Patricia had ignored and mistreated them. Maria was convinced that Patricia and Anne were speaking badly about her and Elizabeth. The entire conversation sounded like something that would come out of the mouth of a second-grader, not a mother and a grandmother.

Patricia stood in shock as Maria spoke. After listening to her unfounded accusations, she finally spoke up to defend herself. She tried to explain that she was grieving the loss of her dog and dealing with the worries of a healthy second pregnancy. But her words fell on deaf ears. It was not what Maria wanted to hear.

Patricia turned to look at Elizabeth and tried to reason with her, but Elizabeth walked out of the room. She claimed to have observed the same behavior. By now, Patricia was growing angry and recalled when her mother would falsely accuse her and behave in a petty manner when she was younger. Maria also walked out of the room.

Patricia exploded, tired of the constant unfounded accusations and assumptions, jealousy, and lack of compassion. They were delusional. Her mother was upset that she had other people in her life that she loved and admired. That was really what this was about, not about anything else, and she managed to drag Elizabeth into it as well.

Patricia followed her mother out to the kitchen and told her exactly how she felt. She explained the reason for her distance during the trip and pointed out to Maria the lack of compassion she exhibited. It was sad that Patricia had to explain her grief and that it was not evident to her mother. But worse, instead of asking what was wrong, she assumed it was a plot against her. Patricia went on to tell her mother that her reactions were that of a spoiled toddler and not of a caring mother. The yelling ensued and came to a point where Armando asked them to step outside as they were disrupting everyone else's evening.

Patricia went outside. Art watched the incident and tried to talk to Maria, pleading with her to calm down and be rational. But Maria was not going to be oblique; she had an audience, and she was going to be heard.

Maria followed Patricia outside and began yelling, "You are an ungrateful brat that only thinks of themselves. You don't ever think of everything I have sacrificed for you and your siblings. If it weren't for me, you would never be where you are now. I got you that job at the airline."

Patricia was growing angrier by the moment. "You've done nothing but hold me back and make it impossible for me to be happy. There is no pleasing you. All you do is cause pain in my life. There can never be a pleasant family gathering because you have to ruin it. This is not about a trip, and you know it. Ever since I was a child, you tried to keep me inside so I would have no friends. As I got older, you continued to keep me from making friends or having a social life. You are jealous that I have moved on and made a life for myself different than the one you lived, and instead of being happy for me, you resent me and want to bring me down and lock me up again. It is not going to work."

By now, Tony had joined them outside and tried to calm the two down. Patricia looked at Tony, trying to get empathy from him and hoping he would echo her words. Tony had his fair run-ins with his mother and was trying to stay out of the argument.

Maria looked at Tony, demanding, "Tell her! Tell her she is wrong and has always disrespected our family!"

Tony could no longer hold his tongue. "Mom, you instigate and are not capable of being happy. You're looking for something to go wrong, to call us out on it. It is hard being your child." And with that, he walked back inside.

Patricia was now exhausted, and the situation was only growing more intense. However, she did not want to ruin everyone's Christmas, so she decided to leave. She drove home, leaving everyone else behind, in hopes it would ease the situation. Luckily, they had taken two cars, and Art and Elise were able to stay and enjoy the rest of the night.

Elizabeth never came out to see what was happening or intervene.

Once again, Patricia felt she was falling back into the same situation that made her dislike the holidays. Why were things just so complicated? At that point, she had determined that she was not to blame. Instead, Maria misplaced her behavior and anger and dragged everyone else into her mess.

Months went by, and Maria never made an effort to reach out, apologize, or make peace. Patricia reached out to Elizabeth and explained her side of the story as she did not want to drive a wedge between them. Elizabeth seemed to understand but was still jaded from Maria's comments, which were hard to ignore. Elizabeth also relied a lot on Maria, so she could not afford to take sides.

"I ask you one question. Do you really believe that as a grown woman, I would talk about my mother and sister behind their backs for no reason?" Patricia asked the question in disbelief.

"Does not make sense," answered Elizabeth.

At this point, time would either heal all wounds or create a bigger divide, but Patricia would not take responsibility for Maria's actions. She would rather do without Maria than tolerate her abusive behavior.

CHAPTER 35

The Party Must Go On

The day came for the new baby to make their appearance. Patricia woke up in the middle of the night and felt wetness in the bed. She got up and raced to the bathroom, realizing her water had broken. Waking Art up, she panicked and thought of Elise but quickly recalled she was at sleep away camp.

They grabbed Patricia's bag and rushed to the hospital. Thankfully, this experience was so different from her first time. She was prepped and wheeled into the delivery room. Hours later, there was baby boy Samuel. He was small, a mere four pounds, eight ounces. Contrary to Elise, Samuel instantly latched on and ate. He was healthy and happy, and that's all that mattered.

On the way to the hospital, Art called Maria to tell her that Patricia was in labor. At this point, they were still not speaking. Maria put her pride aside and made it to the hospital, arriving in time to make it into the delivery room and be the first to meet Samuel.

There was just one slight problem. Elise was supposed to come home the next day from camp, and the day after was her birthday party. Patricia had promised her a dance party with a DJ, which was planned a week before Samuel's arrival. Unfortunately, nobody notified Samuel, and he came a week earlier than expected. Remembering how she felt when Elizabeth was born, she wanted to make sure Elise still felt special.

They had Art's parents pick up Elise from camp, and they came to the hospital. It was the most gratifying sight to see Elise holding her baby brother. She was so sweet. Patricia knew right then and there that Elise would be a wonderful big sister. Patricia spoke to the doctor about leaving the hospital the following day after delivering. Her doctor found it unusual but gave the okay since everything was in order. So, sure enough, Samuel was born at 10 a.m. on July 11th, and they left the hospital at 10 a.m. on July 12th.

As soon as they got home, they began decorating for the party. They had shirts made with the dance party theme in neon pink and blue, and there was a red carpet that led from the driveway to the front door. With Samuel in tow, they accessorized the living room with disco balls, balloons, and removed the furniture to make room for all the dancers. The DJ played top pop music from Elise's playlist. Patricia greeted guests as they arrived, and a photographer snapped pictures as if he was a paparazzi.

The party was a success. Elise had a great birthday, and baby Samuel slept. Everything seemed to be moving in the right direction. Elise was getting ready to go into the third grade, and popularity was significant at that age. Patricia knew that being popular was not necessary but also remembered how being left out was so terrifying. Elise was nothing like Patricia as a child. Not only was she intelligent, but she was also talented and athletic, making the gymnastics trampoline and tumbling team and competing statewide while taking first place in every competition.

All Patricia wanted was to give her kids the best life possible. She felt she had achieved it thus far with Elise, as she seemed to be in good spirits, grateful for her baby brother, and overall demonstrated happiness. But on occasion, Patricia would look over at Elise during her gymnastics competition and catch Elise sucking her lips. She would do this to the point that her lips would swell and become irritated. When Patricia asked her about it, she would deny doing it. Only her lips told a different story. Patricia decided to ask Lindy, "Have you noticed nervousness with Elise when she competes?" "You mean the sucking on her lips?" replied Lindy. "Yes!" Patricia answered in surprise. "I've seen it more and more often," Lindy replied with concern. "I'll keep an eye on it."

Maybe a vacation is in order, thought Patricia. The summer was about to end, and they could all use some fresh air. So they decided to take a road trip to Colorado and leave Lindy to house-sit. Two days into the trip, Patricia got a call. It was Lindy. She was crying and upset.

"What's wrong?" asked Patricia.

Agitated and out of breath, Lindy proceeded to inform Patricia that her girlfriend, who she had just broken up with, came by in the night and smashed Patricia's car windows and cut her tires. Unable to understand what she had to do with Lindy's ex-girlfriend's anger, she decided not to ask and let Lindy finish her story.

Lindy's girlfriend was upset that Lindy had stayed at their home, assuming they were abetting her and lashed out at Patricia's car in revenge. If that wasn't bad enough, Lindy told her ex-girlfriend that she was moving to Portland to get away from her. Patricia was speechless. Lindy was not only their nanny, but she had become part of the family. But Patricia couldn't stand in the way of what Lindy needed to do.

Now Patricia faced the dilemma of finding someone new. Elise was not on board with a new nanny. She begged Patricia to stay home with her and Samuel instead. Patricia promised to try and make it happen but needed to find a replacement in the meantime.

Luckily, their old nanny was available and could help with Samuel. Unfortunately, she did not drive, so Patricia began to work from home and drive Elise to her activities. During this time, Elise's anxiety became more apparent. She was hesitant to go into the gym and wanted to sit in the car until practice started. She was apparently afraid that people were going to criticize her for her skills. She also started to become hyper-aware of her body image.

Patricia decided it was time to talk to Elise about her body and allow her to speak about her self-esteem and ask questions or clear up any doubts she may have.

Patricia took Elise on a walk so they could talk in private. Patricia began to explain to Elise the changes that would take place in her body and speak to her about the origin of babies. Elise listened, and when Patricia finished, Elise informed her that the girls in school talked about these things, but the information they had given her was different. Patricia assured her, "My information is correct. I'm here for you, and if you need to talk about anything, don't hesitate to ask."

Elise replied, "Why do you and Dad fight so much?"

Patricia felt stunned. It was true, but she never really thought Elise noticed. Horrified by the words she heard, Patricia remembered all the fights her mother and father had and how she swore her own kids would never experience that. In her mind, Patricia was shielding Elise.

Patricia apologized to Elise for having experienced this and went on to explain. "Sometimes moms and dads don't agree on everything and get excited when they are disagreeing. But you should not be privy to this. I will do better." Elise was right; Patricia and Art were constantly bickering and disagreeing. Art was more distant than ever, and Patricia was feeling the weight of managing everything at home on her own. When she would try and talk to him about the situation, he would tell her she was making things up and that it was not reality. Patricia wondered if she was overly sensitive about Art's actions based on her past experiences.

Elise had a competition coming up on a Friday night. It was in Dallas, Texas, a four-hour drive from Houston. Patricia drove with Elise and Samuel, and Art would meet them the following day. On the first day of the competition, Patricia noticed Elise's heavy breathing and sucking on her bottom lip. So Patricia tried to help her by showing her meditation exercises to calm her mind before competing.

They seemed to work based on her second round of exercises.

Meanwhile, they expected Art Saturday morning, but he never showed. Instead, Patricia received a message saying a work meeting detained him and that he would come in the afternoon. The afternoon went by with no sign of Art. He finally showed up at close to 8:00 p.m. Patricia and the kids were in the hotel lobby when he arrived. Having just finished dinner, the kids were playing before going to bed. He spotted them, jovially walked over, and kissed them all. Patricia noticed he was swaying back and forth, and his speech was rapid. Something was off.

Patricia took Art aside. "Are you alright? You've missed most of the competition, and your behavior is erratic. Surely you did not drive here drinking?" Art became defensive and denied any wrongdoing. "I was attending a work function and had a few drinks. Don't blow things out of proportion." Patricia did not want to exacerbate the situation as the children were around, and she did not want to create more tension for Elise.

Putting the situation aside, the next day, they finished the competition. There was no more mention of the incident, but it left Patricia uneasy. They all drove back to Houston to continue their routine, only now, Patricia felt that her trust was misplaced.

A couple of months went by, and Art was coming home later and later, and drinking more and more. Every time Patricia would try to talk to him, he would tell her it was all in her imagination. He was guarded and did not want to share his whereabouts, making the relationship even more strained. Patricia was starting to feel pressured to make changes for her and the kids.

Tension in the house started building, and Elise began having night terrors. She would sleepwalk and cry out that someone was attacking her. The night terrors began to worsen, and Patricia worried that Elise could hurt herself by falling down the stairs or hitting her head during one of her fits. To make matters worse, while Elise was having the night terrors, Samuel was also crying in his crib at the same time. The cries were different from that of a child crying out of frustration. They were cries of desperation.

Patricia decided to confide in a friend that had practiced clairvoyance. On a morning walk, she told her what was happening. Her friend said it sounded like unwanted spirits in her house, and if she wanted to clear them out, she would have to follow her instructions. Patricia wondered if it all tied back to the arguing and bad energy coming out of the relationship between her and Art. Nonetheless, she was willing to try whatever she could to stop the horrific nightly routine.

Her friend gave her a chant and instructions. "Grab Elise while she is sleepwalking and hold her tight, all while chanting, 'Go away, you are not wanted here.'" Patricia listened intensely. "As you do this," continued her friend, "you must repeat it over and over until she awakes."

As far-fetched as this sounded to her, Patricia had nothing to lose. So, the next time Elise was walking around in terror and Samuel screamed, Patricia got up from her bed and grabbed Elise, holding her tight. She repeated the chant over and over until, suddenly, she felt a force push them apart. They both fell to the ground, and Elise woke up. Samuel stopped crying. Elise was stunned and did not recall anything.

"Why am I on the floor?" asked Elise. "We were ridding ourselves of unwanted visitors," answered Patricia.

It was the last time Elise ever had a night terror or walked in her sleep again.

CHAPTER 36

The End of an Era

Now a mother of two, Patricia began to evaluate her life. She had gotten to where she was with dedication and persistence, but she had lost sight of what was essential and had made life a race. With Samuel now in her life and Elise getting older, she had to prioritize what was most important to her. Patricia knew that she would have to keep traveling if she stayed at her job, which was not an option. Life had given her what she wanted, and to waste it would be a shame—having enjoyed work and traveling, now it was time to nurture. She remembered the promise she had made to Elise and decided to make a change. Only, in the back of her head, she played out the insecurities and inconsistencies her marriage now presented.

Patricia spoke to Art about her decision to leave work. She also expressed her concern about their marriage. Art assured Patricia that nothing was going on and that he would make an effort to spend more time with family and share in the responsibilities.

With much emotion and doubt, Patricia wrote her resignation letter and presented it to Sam. He was not a man that understood commitment to family or sacrifice for others. He was a selfish person, only looking to see how he could further enjoy life. Unfortunately, Patricia could no longer provide him with a setup to continue frivolously traveling while she worked and sacrificed.

Sam's reaction was blunt. Without emotion, he accepted her resignation and carried on. He mentioned he already had a replacement.

"The company needs a fresh start," he responded. Any doubts she had of leaving were put aside soon after. Patricia's departure was necessary for her mental growth. Only, there was the matter of shares she had earned in her tenure there. The shares caused concern for him. Patricia knew it would be challenging and requested a smooth transition, but money was a priority for Sam, and he would do everything to keep what he had.

Patricia thought of Sam as a father figure. She had worked hard to help him build the business and needed him to be fair while acknowledging that she had been an asset. Expecting him to give her recognition but realizing he was not capable, Patricia proceeded with her departure and began the process of dissolving their partnership and getting paid for what she deserved.

Their relationship did not end well, and just like that, all the years they had shared were gone. Their company's corporate lawyer had to get involved, and Sam spent years threatening to sue Patricia. She once again felt disappointed by someone she admired and loved.

Her children, an insecure marriage to Art, and the failing relationship with Sam triggered her to look for Antonio. She had heard he was back in town, and she wanted to see him. Her need for recognition and acceptance was in full force. She imagined confronting him about what he had done. She wanted him to take responsibility. Now free of work, she researched and discovered he worked across town as a used car salesman. He had taken ill and stopped drinking for a while, and Jen had moved back to Houston to be with him. It was mind-blowing. How could she return to him after all he had done to her?

As the story goes, he had made his way back from Guatemala after the heat was off of him. The police officer in question was gone. Antonio had nowhere to go and found a used car lot, convinced the owner to let him run the dealership, and rent him a home nearby. He had not lost his charm. He was still wheeling and dealing. His daughter, Marlo, was now in college and would come to visit every break. At least one family member stuck with him. *People don't change*, thought Patricia. *Only their circumstances change.* It wouldn't be long before they would all be disappointed once again.

To her surprise, she learned that Tony had visited Antonio. Tony was also looking for closure, but he never got it. Patricia learned from Tony that Antonio did not acknowledge any wrongdoing and, quite the opposite, denied being a terrible father. In Antonio's eyes, his family had treated him with disrespect and had no appreciation for him. Tony also mentioned that Antonio had called Maria when he had nowhere to go—still asking to come back and borrow money. After listening to the story, Patricia decided that seeing Antonio would not give her satisfaction. It had now been 27 years since she last saw him. The closure would need to come from within her. She decided to forgive him for his abuse at that moment, but she would never forget.

Art had a work trip to Germany where he was going to be speaking at a conference in Berlin. Patricia decided to go with him and make it a couples trip. *Maybe we can rekindle the relationship.* After all, they had always enjoyed Berlin when she had to go there for work. The conference was for three days, and they were going for five days. They decided to make it a short trip, as they were leaving the children behind.

Art was charming, and people took to him at the conference. He was knowledgeable on his subject and showed it. Patricia sat in on his sessions to see him in action. It was a good trip. They were having a good time and decided to go to one of their favorite oyster bars they frequented on their past trips. As they were making their way up the escalator, Sam was making his way down. That's right. She ran into Sam in Berlin, of all places. *What are the chances?*, she thought to herself.

Patricia avoided eye contact, but Art ran down the electric stairs and ran up the other side to catch him, all while yelling his name. Patricia wanted to run in the opposite direction. She slowly walked up to meet them, but Sam made no eye contact and refused to even look at her. Surprisingly, Sam proceeded to engage in conversation with Art and exchange niceties. Not sure what to make of the meeting, she was perplexed that Art would engage with Sam knowing how she felt about him. But she remained silent, and they walked away after Art and Sam finished their conversation.

Their trip ended with a traditional German dinner and men dancing in Lederhosen while drinking beer. Despite the run-in with Sam, the trip had been surreal, and she had loved spending time alone with Art. But she was ready to go home to the kids.

Now back home, Patricia was having a hard time adjusting to not working. She had worked in some capacity since the age of 12. She loved spending time with the kids, but there was only so much she could do. Elise was in school, and Samuel was attending a mother's day out program. He was now a year old and needed interaction.

Patricia decided she would take the downtime and focus on her relationship with Art. Maybe if she showed him a kinder side of herself, he would come around. Their relationship had deteriorated; they were not co-parenting, nor were they partners. Art did his own thing, and she basically took on all the day-to-day responsibilities. She could live with him working all the time, but when he did take a break, he was irritable, impatient, and critical. Patricia had managed to ignore the behavior as she was busy with her career and family, but now that she had more time to reflect, she noticed Art's indifference.

Patricia cooked special meals for the family to eat together, kept the house clean, and tried not to get in Art's way, allowing him to work as much as possible. At one point, they had come to an agreement. Art would cut off working at six o'clock and spend two hours with the family before returning to work. Unfortunately, this arrangement only lasted a month before things went back to their old ways.

Patricia struggled with both her present and past. She was doubtful of herself, always thinking that her feelings were not about Art and the way he treated her. They were buried feelings about her father. She began to go back to therapy, and during her sessions, she began to see how Art's dismissal of her feelings was partially to blame for her confusion between the past and the present. Art had some knowledge of her childhood, and he would use it occasionally to justify his behavior. Patricia knew she needed to work on letting go of the past and focusing on the present. But the present was intertwined with deception and secrets that felt similar to her past.

Art was always very guarded about his whereabouts and his personal life, even after being married, but now things seemed so distant that Patricia began to wonder what he was doing on his trips away. She hoped she was wrong, but her intuition was strong.

CHAPTER 37

Breaking Cycles

With her marriage on the rocks, Patricia thought it best to focus on her connection with her family. Unfortunately, her relationship with Maria remained fractured. She felt that Maria was manipulative and when things did not go her way, she would talk about whoever she was mad at with one of the other kids, causing anxiety and rifts among the siblings. Patricia was unsure if this was intentional or not, but it was certainly toxic.

Maria loved being a grandmother but loved being a martyr even more. When asked to babysit, she would do it, but not without first making comments and complaints that she was not appreciated or demanding special attention. Soon, Patricia learned not to ask, preferring to hire outside help. Maria received invites to visit or have dinner, but Patricia would not allow her mother to manipulate her.

Patricia tried to be understanding with her mother, realizing Maria had many obstacles to fight through as a child and as an adult. No one had taught her true love, but Patricia found it hard to accept that her mother did not move forward to change her circumstances even as she got older and had access to more resources.

Tired of the constant conflict that had always ruled her family, Patricia decided to take control of the relationship between her brother and sister. She spoke to them one at a time and shared her thoughts on the behavior she had witnessed. They made a pact never to assume that the words said by Maria were 100% true. Instead, they agreed to always ask and check in with each other and not harbor ill will among the three of them. It was a significant turning point for them in building a healthy relationship.

Ultimately, it was up to each of them to break the cycles that had been playing out for generations. Elizabeth was still in a lousy marriage, living her terror in silence. But, painful as it was, Patricia knew she needed to be accessible for her sister on Elizabeth's terms. Patricia valued her little sister in so many ways that it was hard to believe there was ever any doubt that she would not love her. Beautiful and successful, it wouldn't be long before Elizabeth would find her way and seek happiness.

Armando's behavior only worsened with time, continually treating Elizabeth with disrespect. Patricia insisted that Elizabeth believe in herself and not tolerate Armando's belligerent behavior any longer. It was not only a terrible way for her to live, but it was a horrible example for her children. Armando would go out three to four days a week, staying out late and coming home intoxicated. Elizabeth did not protest, as she enjoyed not having him around. She was the most lenient wife ever. No one else would have put up with his shenanigans.

As time went on, he became more and more aggressive, and Elizabeth was starting to tire of the behavior. She had to travel more and more for work, and Armando began to project his infidelity on

Elizabeth, claiming *she* was unfaithful. Finally, Elizabeth had enough and called it quits. She informed Armando she would be filing for a divorce. He was caught off-guard and felt as if he had been side-swiped. Their split was torturous, but she was finally free of him. After that, Armando began to spin out of control and ended up having a stroke and became incapacitated. It was hard for everyone, especially the children.

Years went by, and he never fully recovered. He was unable to walk and had to relearn to talk. Feeling regretful, Armando called Elizabeth to express how he felt. "I've been reflecting on the family I lost and let down, and I want to express my remorse. I wish I could get the time back, but I've learned that time does not give back. It only takes. Please forgive me." With pain in her voice, Elizabeth accepted his apology. Elizabeth forgave Armando, realizing he was suffering his consequence while watching everyone move on. It must have been a living hell for him.

With Armando out of the picture, good fortune came for Elizabeth. She was now free of unnecessary distractions and obstacles, earning her a promotion at work. Elizabeth started to find herself; trying to become a stronger, more confident woman. But she still had one major challenge, just like Patricia. Elizabeth needed to break the pattern of attracting the wrong people in her life. She was working towards that and wanted to show her daughter, Kate, to be strong.

Maria was critical of Elizabeth taking pity on Armando and now making him the victim. Elizabeth did not feel like her mother was supportive, and rightfully so. It was a complete contradiction. Yes, Maria was there to help with the kids now that Elizabeth was a single mom, but it was always with a judging eye. Maria criticized everything Elizabeth did. The way she parented, how much she worked, her spending—the list was endless. It was just like when Elizabeth was a child. There was never unconditional love or empathetic support, only judgment and criticism. Maria never acknowledged Elizabeth's successes or expressed how proud she was. It was hard for Elizabeth, who only desired approval.

Kate was resilient and intelligent and, just like her mother, a straight-A student. The emotional stress of the family dynamic was not easy on her and her brother, but they managed. Despite her father's behavior, Kate was close to Armando, as he would talk to her and relate to her on a more juvenile level than her mother. Overall, the balance would have been fine if it weren't for her father's abusive personality. When Kate would choose not to visit him or call him, he would threaten to cut her off financially or take away her car, always holding something over her. Kate found it hard to see her father in his current condition, so she avoided him as much as possible. She didn't do it out of harm or dislike, just simply out of preservation of her sanity.

Patricia loved Kate very much and wished she could help her but did not know how, other than reaching out to check in on her and offer her support. With the family dynamics, it was hard for Patricia to help Kate without feeling like she was overstepping boundaries. Kate felt that people were prying and trying to put her in the middle of her parents' battles.

Kate would soon go off to college and make her way through life. Patricia's hope and wishes for her were for her to be free of pain and relinquish any undeserved responsibilities to her parents. Patricia knew all too well that when the people around them aren't held accountable for their actions, the blame becomes misplaced onto the victim.

As for her younger brother, Finn, he had inherited his dad's ability to smile and put on a front despite the pain he endured. He was a loving boy who cared dearly for his mother. Finn would put Elizabeth's feelings ahead of his own. Even at such a young age, he had already decided that he was responsible for her happiness. He also loved his father and cherished the moments they shared. Finn was consistent, making sure to visit his dad regularly.

While you are assigned a family at birth, friendships are earned through unconditional love. Finn and Samuel were not only cousins but friends. Samuel looked up to Finn, and Finn was kind and loving to Samuel. It made Patricia happy to see that her kids had a family to support them and be there for them. She hoped they would remain good friends as she and her sister had when they got older.

Then there was Tony, who never married. He had two children he dedicated his time to, along with growing his business. Patricia wondered if he ever knew how much she appreciated his companionship as a child or if he knew how special he was. To overcome constant negativity and abuse and become a self-made success was no small feat. So often, she looked at him and saw in his sad eyes the need for approval and acknowledgment of his success from the two people who would never provide it, because they were not capable.

Tony tried to find peace with Maria, but they always ended up arguing. Without knowing it, Tony wanted to punish Maria, angry about the past and the present. He felt like she repeated the same behavior, never learning from her experiences. Even though Tony continually tried to distance himself from his mother, something always kept them together.

One year, Hurricane Harvey forced Tony and Maria together; one of the worst storms to hit Houston. There had been so many storm warnings throughout the years, as Houston was always in the path of most hurricanes, but they usually fizzled out; this one didn't seem to be changing course.

The storm was worse than anyone imagined, bringing 51 inches of rain and winds of 100 miles per hour. Objects flew, and the surges left most of the area underwater. Many of Tony's neighbors were evacuating, but Tony refused, claiming people were overreacting. Everyone pleaded with him to vacate, but to no avail. Luckily, his youngest son was off at college, and his older son was married and safe with his family.

Tony's home got destroyed by the hurricane. Elizabeth took him in, where he remained for a couple of weeks until she politely asked him if he planned on finding other accommodations. Unsure of what he would do, Tony moved in with Maria, who had an extra bedroom.

He did not plan to stay long, but ended up living with his mother for three years.

The time he spent living with Maria was tough. Barring a few good moments, they mostly argued. Tony had a lot of resentment towards Maria, and living with her stirred up many long-held emotions. The majority of their fights stemmed from differences in their recollections.

Maria would always bring up the past to Tony. "I remember all the times I defended you from your dad and kept you safe."

Tony would reply, "I don't remember feeling safe, and we stayed in that house for too long."

"If it weren't for me, you would never have success," she would recite back like a broken record.

Tony would answer in anger, "I am successful on my own accord, no thanks to you or my father. I did it all on my own."

The incidents they both experienced were the same, but their interpretation was different—both their perceptions and the way they recalled the incidents were engraved in their minds. Tony finally moved out, allowing them both some peace.

Tony had many obstacles and roadblocks that made him navigate life differently than most people. But one thing he was able to accomplish was raising two kids who were go-getters. Both boys achieved exceptional successes. He felt honored to be their father and tried to show them his continuous support and pride. He went above and beyond as a father, covering his own need for validation that he never received.

In addition to rebuilding his business, Tony began a non-profit, giving back to the community where he grew up. He helped inner-city young men prepare for college and adulthood by steering them in the right direction to be productive individuals who contribute to society.

Tony still watched over his sisters, even if they were all grown. He checked in on them as well as his nephews and nieces. He worried about their well-being and their choices when picking a partner.

Armando and Tony were never close when he was married to Elizabeth, but later, after his medical problems, Armando would ask Tony for help, as he knew he could rely on him. Tony never held a grudge and was always there to help in any way he could. Tony was relieved that Elizabeth was free from the toxic relationship but did not judge Armando on his past.

As for Art, Tony was fond of him. He knew Art was brilliant and liked his wit. "Only highly intelligent people can understand Art. His sarcasm is not for everyone," Tony would say after having a conversation with him. Tony did not get involved in Patricia's relationship, as he knew Patricia was private, but he always wondered if she was truly happy.

CHAPTER 38

A Ghost From the Past

Years had gone by, and Patricia did not have any interaction with her father. Tony would occasionally seek him out and randomly inform Elizabeth and Patricia about his interactions with Antonio. In addition, Tony did keep up with their half-sister, Marlo, trying to build a relationship with her. He always saw himself as the conduit in keeping the family together.

One day, out of the blue, Tony got a call from his cousin, Antonio's sister's daughter. She informed him that Antonio had been diagnosed with terminal cancer. Apparently, he had colon cancer that had spread to three other areas. Tony hung up the phone, and sadness silently came over him. He felt that he would never have closure for the past, but he was not one to feel sorry for himself and decided to call Antonio's wife and see what was happening.

Tony called Jen to find out the details. Jen was vague as she did not have a lot of information at the moment. They had been in Philadelphia for her mother's funeral when Antonio began to feel sick, unable to eat or go to the bathroom. It got to the point that Antonio passed out and went to the hospital for testing, where they gave him the diagnosis. They returned home but had not made it to the doctor in Houston for further testing and next steps.

Tony called each of his sisters to give them the news. He intended to visit Antonio, offer his help, and encourage each of them to do the same. Only, they were not as inclined to follow his lead. Elizabeth responded that she had not seen Antonio in years and that it did not seem that he was asking to see her, so it felt hypocritical to reach out now.

Patricia heard Tony out, and as he was speaking, she recalled when she got the call that Antonio had been in a car accident, and she and her family rushed to the hospital to be supportive and offer help. However, she recalled the outcome of Antonio throwing her mother out of the hospital and using Maria to help him recover, only to return to his nasty ways. While Patricia felt compassion for what Antonio was going through now, she did not see how she could help him and as Elizabeth pointed out, he was not asking for them.

For a moment, Patricia imagined herself going to Antonio, talking and getting insight into why he did the things he did, but she quickly came to her senses. Her father would never own his part in their past. He would only turn it back to him being misunderstood and having unappreciative children.

Antonio had surgery to remove his colon upon his return to Houston and suddenly reported that everything was okay. He did not have to endure any other procedures, chemo, or radiation. Tony continued to follow up with his father and was shocked to hear the news. Puzzled about how he went from widespread cancer to being cured with one surgery, he was skeptical of the truth. But this was consistent with Antonio's flow of information.

Patricia recalled her mother's words, "Bad seeds never die." Not that she wished Antonio any harm, but how could he overcome such a severe diagnosis when people they knew, *good* people, had passed away, having fewer complications? Only time would tell if he was indeed out of danger. But for the moment, Patricia figured maybe he had been given additional time to reflect on his past.

The incident did stir up conversations between Maria and Patricia. Maria expressed her sorrow that she thought everyone blamed her for the incidents that took place when they were children. Especially Tony. She felt that she was a victim and that everyone had pity for Antonio, while she was left dealing with the aftermath.

Maria never took responsibility for her part in the chaos, and she continued with the same toxic patterns, even as her children were well into their adult lives and had children of their own. She never recognized her role or tried to change her reactions and habits to create a healthy family environment. All that her three children ever wanted was for her to love them unconditionally and without judgment, and to acknowledge what they had achieved. They wanted her to be proud of them, that they had found a better life despite the many obstacles. But she was never able to see past herself.

The three loved her in their way. She was kind and giving, but when she did offer her love, it always came with consequences, so they could not show their true appreciation.

Maria lived a sad life, never remarrying and living vicariously through her children. She was a devout Catholic with few friends. Although her struggle was genuine, Maria never dealt with her horrible childhood or the abuse she endured as an adult. Instead, Maria repeated the same patterns her mother had imposed on her, never learning from them.

Maria's relationship with her mother played a significant role in her own mothering. She felt her mother favored her brother, Juan, and never enjoyed or valued her. Unfortunately, Maria's mother never showed her how much she appreciated her, leaving Maria feeling empty. But instead of breaking the cycle, Maria unconsciously repeated the same behavior. Maria supported her mother to the bitter end, making sure she had everything she needed and ensuring she was financially and medically taken care of for life. But the resentment stayed with her.

The little girl who was rejected from her family was reflected and manifested in everything Maria did. Her story was one of abuse and neglect like no other. Most would not have survived. Yet, despite everything, Patricia saw her mother as a true hero and felt empathy for her. But for Maria, she would never find peace.

Patricia reflected that the struggles she had with her mother started before her birth. She recalled a session she had with a shaman on a business trip a couple of years prior. A marketing meeting took place at a resort in Mexico, and when Patricia arrived, the resident shaman came looking for her. She had never met or seen him before.

"Come look for me when you're done," he called out to her. "I can help you with your fear of water." *How does he know about my fears?* "Bring your bathing suit," continued the shaman.

When Patricia finished her meeting, the shaman met her by the pool. He took her by the hands and told her they were going to do water therapy. He gently guided her into the pool. Patricia was nervous, as she did not know this person. He was so mysterious, and at the same time, she felt compelled to do what he said.

"We are going to reconstruct your birth," he repeatedly said as he cradled her in the water back and forth, plunging her in and out, swaying from one side of the pool to the other, spinning her in a circle.

Patricia was in a daze. Her eyes closed tight. In a fetal position, her body felt as though it was floating through a canal. The feeling of drowning would take over her with each plunge, gasping for air and then suddenly receiving it as she came to the surface.

As the session ended, he gently dunked her one last time and placed her on the side of the pool. The shaman patiently waited for her to open her eyes and catch her breath. Then, he reminded Patricia of her traumatic birth, how she had drowned in her mother's womb and had been resuscitated at birth.

"Subconsciously, you have held onto this memory that has caused unresolved issues between yourself, water, and your mother. Forgiveness is necessary to surpass the fears that linger within you."

The session with the shaman shed light on many unresolved issues Patricia harbored, not only with her mother, but also with water. Water was always an element in her struggles.

Patricia always gave her mother credit for having a part in making her and her siblings resilient. Good or bad, they had learned to forge forward, pushing past hardship to find success. The shaman's words resonated with her as she began to let go of her past and learned to love her mother for who she was. Letting go of the anger she harbored felt good and made her empathetic to the struggles her mother faced.

BREAKING SILENCE

Breaking the silence as thoughts rush from
my head and become real

The moment I speak, I begin to feel

The silence, a harmful shield

The words rush out, I shout

I am free just as the bird that spreads its wings, I must be

No shame here, nothing to see

The words rush out, and I grow

Like a vine that wraps its roots now, I'm free to flow

My body and mind let go

Taking in the freshness of air, no more silence I dare

Those who listen beware, you'll live on in my stare

No need to be scared, the words rush out
and break to pieces in the air

Not to harm or beware, just a release to bring me peace

A tranquility merging my mind, body,
and soul as pain cease

Listen to me today, tomorrow, and you'll
hear no more sorrow

I've learned that time we cannot borrow

I choose to live open and proclaim living and loving,
coming out from under the shadow

CHAPTER 39

Finding Balance

Patricia's relationship with Art was deteriorating faster than she could come up with solutions. She was lonely and frustrated. He was not always present, even when he was around. Art was a good man but lacked empathy. Art was haunted by demons that drove him not to trust or open himself to love others. It was demonstrated in his actions towards his family.

He grew up learning that problems were swept under the rug and not spoken of ever. But he had given her two of the most important things in her life—Elise and Samuel. Her children were everything, but she vowed not to make them responsible for her happiness. That was *her* job.

The time came when Patricia needed to make a decision about her future. By now, through lots of soul searching and counseling, she had determined that the feelings she experienced in her marriage were real.

They were not the past, and they were not unfounded. She was only being fooled and gaslit to feel like they were.

Patricia knew she was not perfect, but she also recognized that she was tolerant, and probably more forgiving than most due to her upbringing. But the time had come to be true to herself and her children. Patricia realized that Art was not going to change. He enjoyed living a separate life and having his family around when he needed them. But it was no longer good enough for Patricia. She knew she wanted more. She wanted someone to love her and someone to be her partner; to truly value her for who she was, and Art could not give her that. Art's values and hers were never aligned, but they became even more unbalanced with time. He wanted more and more material things, and Patricia wanted more and more spirituality in her life.

Mother's Day was never a good time since Art had lost his mom. He became irate on the day and resentful. Patricia dreaded the holiday that was supposed to be about celebrating her, as she knew the mood in the house was going to be unpleasant. Art always managed to end the day by having Patricia in tears from his comments and disregard.

That particular Mother's Day was different in that Patricia decided nothing would ruin the day for her. Her sister and mother were in town, and they planned on having dinner together. They would celebrate each other along with the kids. Art noticed no one considered him, and that triggered a negative reaction. Patricia paid no mind, as she knew he was waiting for an opportunity to lash out. However, the more she ignored him, the more he stewed, until he no longer held back. "You and your family think you're so great. You are a bunch of losers. Your mom is always in my way, and your sister is so loud. And let's not get started on how you people treat my things. You scratch the walls when you walk by and scratch my stove when you cook." Art was on a rampage.

Patricia just stared at him and, without a second thought, yelled, "I'm done. I want a divorce. You need to leave." Something snapped. She could no longer take it.

"Fine!" Art yelled with disregard as he grabbed his things and walked out.

Elizabeth and Maria just stared in disbelief. They were aware that Patricia was unhappy, but neither thought she would ever make a decision to split from Art. They offered their support to Patricia and reluctantly made their way back to Houston.

Weeks went by, and Patricia did not hear from Art. He finally came back as if nothing had happened, but she was not having it and did not let him back in. Patricia was determined to move on. As painful as it was, she could no longer take his dismissal. Deep down inside, she still loved Art, but there was no turning back; Patricia had heard his regrets and false promises too often.

Art managed to talk to Patricia and express his side of the story. "I work hard to create a dynasty for our children and provide for the family. I have a lot of resentment towards you because you constantly judge me. What I drink, what I do. I feel unappreciated. But I want to make things right and keep our family together."

Patricia accepted her responsibility for the marriage not working, but it was too late. She knew Art was only telling her what she wanted to hear. He could not keep his promise of spending more time with the family or drinking less or learning to be respectful in his communication. She knew this from the 24 years she had heard the same promises. It was time to trust her intuition and let go.

As they were dissolving the marriage, Patricia continued with therapy, making it a priority in her life—for her sake and the sake of her children. She knew life constantly presented her with challenges, and while no one is born with a manual, using the past as an excuse to navigate the present was inexcusable. Patricia knew she needed to get the tools necessary to become the best she could be. She wanted to break cycles, not add to their destructive nature.

By now, Patricia felt she had lived many lives. She wore many hats: partner, mother, business owner, justice-seeker, but she realized that no one really knew her. Reflecting on her relationships with people made her feel hypocritical. Keeping to herself and wearing a smile for others, she rarely let people see her pain and struggles. Yet, her desire to help others was intense. It was a complex situation, and she pondered on the question, *How can you help others when you cannot face your own truth?*

In addition, now with a teenage daughter, she wanted to show Elise how to be strong and true to herself, teaching her to value who she was. Not having a true sense of how to parent a teenager, Patricia trusted her instincts and remembered all that she disliked about her treatment when she was that age. The things that really stood out were the need for trust, compassion, and the ability to make her own decisions and mistakes.

Patricia treated Elise with respect, being clear about the boundaries and repercussions for mishaps, while at the same time letting her know that if she needed help, she would be there for her, no questions asked, and no judgment. It was a tricky balance, but it was what would work for them.

Unfortunately, Art did not follow the same doctrine. Instead, he began to treat Elise with the same disrespect and disregard as he had done with Patricia. Art's relationship with Elise worsened, pushing her further and further away. Art was incapable of recognizing the toxic atmosphere he created and expected his children to dwell in during their visits. It was an uphill battle, but one Patricia would need to learn to rise above while helping Elise and Samuel decipher falsehood from reality.

With her kids becoming more and more independent and Art out of her day-to-day, Patricia became bored and started to think of different businesses she could create. She was an entrepreneur by nature. Having spent years in the tourism industry, but wanted to get out. The industry had been good to her, and she had enjoyed many privileges and benefits, but it was time to move on and do something more substantial.

She brainstormed on using her marketing skills, her desire to help others, and her mastery of creating a business, and came up with an idea to help women struggling to develop their own identities. Patricia had seen mothers and partners left in the dust, struggling to recreate their lives as family life changed. She had friends with many degrees that gave up their careers to raise their families and support their husbands' growth in their jobs. As life evolved and the children went to college or faced divorce, these women had no actual work history and were left to figure out how to make a living. Technically, they were too old to enter the workforce again and had no recent work experience.

Patricia revived her marketing site and began to create How-To-Start-Up-Marketing kits. Her goal was to allocate a percentage of the kits for women who had little resources to get their lives back up and running—giving them the power to lift themselves up, hire others, and give them an opportunity to be independent. She was creating a paying-it-forward cycle.

Patricia was unsure of its feasibility but felt it was right. She was determined to push forward with it. After all, she created something with passion and fulfilled her desire to give more than she would receive. It was a great start to giving back.

Patricia realized that everything she had endured in life was for a reason. She had learned many skills and appreciated the lessons that made her the woman she had become. For the first time, pride started to manifest, and the fears and insecurities buried within her began to shed. Patricia was emerging as a more positive and brighter version of herself. It was her time to shine and let people see who she really was. No longer would she hide behind someone and let them put out her light.

She thought about her nieces and nephews and how they never knew the true story of their family and what was behind their parents struggles. She wondered if learning about their family's past and hearing their childhood stories would help them understand and break any imposed cycles. Only, she did not know how to share the stories with them. After all, they were intense and impactful, and they couldn't just be brought up in conversation. It was, again, another part of her healing.

Patricia had everything in her to tell the story. One day, while taking a writing class, she began to write and didn't stop until she wrote her memoir. The words poured out, and the memories rushed to the pages. Her journey began to be transparent and healing. Patricia learned her past was indeed in the past, but began to recognize repeated patterns in her life before splitting with Art. She had a notion of them, but her memories and reality lived in parallel. Writing her memoir brought her to the "Aha!" moment. Once the truth revealed itself, she became confident in her choice and began living her best life.

Though it felt as if her memoir came about by accident, Patricia wondered if that really was the case. Instead, maybe it was just the way it was supposed to happen. Had she come to a point in her life where she had enough knowledge and experience to move forward with her real purpose?

As a child, she always questioned her existence. She felt there had to be more to her than just another body taking up space. Patricia knew she had many more lessons to learn. Still, she felt she was on the right path for the first time in her life. Something bigger than herself was pushing her in an unfamiliar direction, but Patricia felt safe and healthy. Most importantly, she was opening spaces for others to follow their dreams, break the silence, and live their most authentic, joyful life.

About the Author

I started off writing this book so that the abuse, pain, and suffering my family and I lived through and with would no longer be pushed down and ignored. I chose to write it in a third-person perspective because I always saw myself as an outsider looking in. It was my coping mechanism; the way my mind protected me. But I was tired of being silenced. So, I lifted the veil, hoping to help others who suffered or are still suffering abuse.

Most people don't know me. I build barriers that protect me, not allowing very many people inside. I share minimally, and I don't walk around telling people how I grew up. So, as you can imagine, this was not an easy task to put it all out there for everyone to read. This book is about my perception of the feelings and experiences I endured. My brother and sister, the characters in the book, all have different views on how things occurred. Each of us lived our own personal nightmare. However, we all agree on one thing: it was toxic and unbearable.

I remembered incidents I had forgotten while writing the story and gained a different perspective from things as I remembered them. I learned a lot about myself and why I do things. In my world, it's black and white, and people are either good or bad. There is no in-between. I'm always suspicious and never take things for their face value. Right or wrong, these are the instincts that I developed as a child.

Therapy is a big part of my life, and every day, I get stronger, as I learn more and more about myself. I was an insecure woman who did not love herself; afraid to be alone and begging for attention. I am not that woman anymore. I can honestly say I love myself. I am no longer afraid to be alone and realize that I am my own best company. Once I learned to love myself, I began to love others.

I am far from perfect, but I am self-aware of my downfalls. Every once in a while, I cycle through the emotions buried deep in my mind. I get depressed, want to give up, get angry, and become self-loathing, but I know the feelings will pass. So, I acknowledge them and just keep on moving. Recognizing those feelings and emotions makes them less powerful; not allowing them to grow and take over.

I am not a medical professional, but from my experience, I have concluded that specific traumas in my life left deep scars. Even if I tried to bury them, they survived in my subconscious. Certain people were able to pick up on the vulnerability I created and take advantage of it. I often would question why things happened to me or why things *kept* happening, but it wasn't until I learned self-love and self-respect that the vulnerability disappeared.

During my childhood, I always felt that someone was watching over me, taking care of me. It was a feeling I could not explain. I like to think of it as my adult self, looking after me to ensure that the child within me met the woman I would eventually become. My road was destined to push forward, one that was meant to help others along the way—giving light and hope. I don't regret the things that happened. I embrace them. They are what made me who I am today.

I helped build and make four companies successful. I am a mother of two exceptional children. My oldest daughter is incredible; she shines her beauty inside and out. She is more than I could have hoped to have and is the reason I am still here. She gives me hope every day and inspires me to be better. I want to be her when I grow up. My son is witty and challenges me to teach him to express himself and be confident, constantly keeping me on my toes. We share a special bond, and his presence lights up my heart. I could not love either one more.

I started my mission to heal and gain all the tools possible to be mentally healthy for them. I wanted to be the best parent I could be, giving them love and stability. I make mistakes and often joke about how I am giving them something to talk about in therapy when they get older. I realized what a big responsibility it is to be a parent. To make sure they are safe and cared for; I am the example they will follow. I need to be a leader.

I chose not to follow my mother's example. Somehow, I knew it was not the right way to live. I took the best parts of her and applied them to my life. She is self-sufficient, never needs anyone, and is a problem-solver. She is still in my life, and I love her dearly. I forgive her lack of knowledge to parent the right way. Still, I don't understand why she continues to live in constant turmoil, never learning to love herself and incapable of understanding others.

My brother and sister and I have built a nurturing and caring relationship while respecting each other. It has not been easy, but we have achieved it. It amazes me how the three of us have survived despite the odds and came out relatively normal and self-aware of our emotional health.

When my son was six months old, I went back to work, consulting until about three months before writing this book. As I divorced Art, I had come to another fork in the road. I decided to be true to myself and follow my passion for helping others and writing. Art and I were oil and water. He lacked the ability to understand and love me for who I was. Art often overlooked the simple things in life, but he helped me grow and pushed me to be more than I could ever have hoped to be, and I will always be grateful to him for that.

I hope to help others. Life is not a simple recipe. It is complicated and forces one to grow beyond their comfort zones. So I put myself out there, because growth is necessary. Everyone needs tools to be able to navigate. And when times get tough, **just keep moving**.

Writing this book, I discovered so many things about myself. What started as a simple project for an online class turned into the most crucial learning tool of my life. It turned my world upside down, and it allowed me to live out all the things I desire: health, happiness, and love. I am opening myself to others and attracting the correct type of people into my inner circle.

I encourage everyone to journal and write. It will help you discover who you are and allow you to heal.

Letter to Little Patricia

Dear Child,

I want to let you know that you will survive. Things will get better for you and your family. You will not live all of your life in the dark. The closet you sit in is just a capsule to insulate the pain. The mind that takes you places is a vessel to open your world and show you light.

Don't despair. There is hope. Take my hand. I will guide you and make sure we meet in the future. There is much work for you to do; this is not all in vain. I know you question, and you have every right to do so. No one should have to endure the pain, the abuse, the neglect. Just remember, it is not your fault. Leave the guilt behind. Let the people who put you in this position own it. It is not yours to take. You are a beautiful person, worthy of love. Unfortunately, you are in a situation with people incapable of giving it to you.

You are a light. You glow. You possess a gift that you will later learn to use. That gift carries you through this childhood and your adulthood. So when you feel the wind caress your skin, it is me reminding you that you're alive. You are not invisible; people see you. But they are not sure of what they see, as you don't reveal yourself. So leave the shame and the embarrassment; they are not worthy of your space. It does not belong to you. It belongs to the people who took it from you.

Don't listen to the negative words spoken to you, telling you are not worthy, that you will never be more than just a hopeless soul destined for a miserable existence. It is just a self-reflection of the people speaking the words. You are capable of so much and deserving of love. Open yourself up, let people into your life, and allow them to see the real you.

Follow your dreams, use your imagination to manifest your destiny, float above the chaos and leave it behind. Then, as you grow older, you will be able to rewrite your story, replacing terrorizing memories with happier ones you have created. That's the beauty of the gift.

This gift you possess is not for everyone. Chosen above everyone else, make sure to use it. You will be the light that guides those around you. You will become overwhelmed, as it is a big task, but it is one you are capable of, or it wouldn't be yours. Don't give up. It'll all be clear when we meet in the future. I am with you always.

Love,
Your future self

Lessons Learned

Throughout my life, I have learned many lessons, and I continue to learn. I have not always been open to taking the experiences and learning from them, but eventually, they become clear. Some of these lessons may just be for me, but others may find them helpful, too.

- Not everything or everyone is as it seems. People can have intentions to do something good, but it unintentionally turns out to be bad. Most people don't just set out to hurt, and thinking with assumptions can cause an emotional rollercoaster.
- Unconditional love is allowing your loved ones to make mistakes free from your judgment.
- Forgiving others for their mistakes is imperative for self-growth. Carrying around resentment and hate only weighs us down, not allowing us to move on.

- When we don't like how things are going, **just keep moving**. Change directions and find a more comfortable path.
- You can make yourself invisible by hiding your feelings and not letting others in.
- You can't properly love others if you don't love yourself first.
- Others won't respect you until you respect yourself.
- Don't wait to be picked or recognized. You have to shout, "I am here."
- Others can't help you if you don't speak up.
- Don't assume people are doing things just to hurt you. Most of the time, they are unaware, or we assign a negative purpose.
- You can rewrite your memories, replacing bad ones with happy ones you created.
- Follow your instinct.
- Living outside your comfort zone and pushing the boundaries will open new worlds.
- Use your words. People need to hear you.
- Mental health is continual and necessary.
- When you bury emotions, they will come back to haunt you.
- Most people never change; their *circumstances* change, so they adapt.
- The things you love about someone when you meet them can eventually be what you dislike about them in the future.
- Don't make assumptions about people until you get to know them.
- Sometimes, the rough times become the best times.
- Love is being able to let people be themselves.
- Don't expect others to be responsible for your happiness; look within.
- Don't let people around you own your success; recognize it and own it for yourself.
- Your possessions do not define you. Instead, they are the barriers that hide you.
- Be grateful even for the tough times, for they are what make you stronger.

- Don't just discard relationships as bad. Thank them for teaching you to be patient.
- Listening is often better than giving your opinion.
- Don't judge a person by their facial expressions; their internal worries or thoughts often take over their reflection, having nothing to do with what they see in you.

Life lessons are ongoing. Situations often come up that challenge us, tear us down, and just when we think we can't make it, we become stronger and rise up again. Reach out to me and speak your truth so that we can learn together. Sharing stories, tears, and fears will help us persevere in living our best life.

Instagram: https://www.instagram.com/beltransandrap/
Facebook: https://www.facebook.com/BeltranSandraP
Website: www.sandrabeltran.com

Let's Stay in Touch:
As I **Keep Moving**, I've created a series of blog posts where I speak my truth and share several coping mechanisms that I use in my own life. For me, speaking my truth is being transparent about the events that made me who I am. It means revealing situations that may be uncomfortable to talk about, but are necessary to live a healthier, happier life.

I started writing my truth in a class, and when the words spilled out on paper, they reminded me of the strengths I had to survive. Before writing my book, my back story, so to speak, was never a topic of conversation. Now, the book compels people to ask questions, and when I do share, many people open up and tell me stories from their past. Many times, I am surprised by what I hear, and it makes me realize that life is full of untold stories.

Speaking the truth is not about assigning blame or becoming part of a movement. It is mainly about clearing your mind of all the cobwebs and damaging tracks buried deep, in those things that keep you from moving forward and becoming the best version of yourself.

You don't have to write a book or spill your guts to everyone you meet to speak your truth. The process is different for everyone. So speak your truth in private or in public, but let go of the mental and emotional roadblocks that don't serve you, and start making room for your best life.

Join my blog and sign up to receive updates: https://www.sandrabeltran.com/blog

Giving Back

Life sometimes takes us outside our comfort zone, especially during significant life changes. Children get older, relationships end, and you or your spouse may lose a job. Women often dedicate their core years to raising their families. When looking to go back into the workforce, they are no longer in their "prime" and are technically not hireable.

Through my marketing company, I have created How-To-Start-Up marketing kits that will help guide people in the right direction, allowing them to create opportunities and become self-sufficient.

As others have helped me, my mission is to pay-it-forward and help others achieve a better life. That's why a percentage of every book sold will go toward creating How-To-Start-Up marketing kits for women who don't have the knowledge or resources to get themselves on their feet.

NOTES

NOTES

NOTES

NOTES

NOTES

NOTES

NOTES

NOTES

www.ingramcontent.com/pod-product-compliance
Lightning Source LLC
Chambersburg PA
CBHW020435130626
46549CB00001B/144